Rick Steves'

GERMAN

Phrase Book & Dictionary

4th Edition

John Muir Publications
Santa Fe, New Mexico

Thanks to the team of people at *Europe Through the Back Door* who helped make this book possible: Dave Hoerlein, Mary Romano, and . . .

German translation: Julia Klimek
Phonetics: Risa Laib
Layout: Rich Sorensen and Colleen Murphy
Maps: David C. Hoerlein

Edited by Risa Laib and Rich Sorensen

John Muir Publications, P.O. Box 613, Santa Fe, NM 87504

Printed in the U.S.A. by Banta Company
Fourth edition. First printing March 1999

ISBN 1-56261-477-0

Cover photos: Neuschwanstein Castle, Bavaria, Germany;
                      © Blaine Harrington III
                      Foreground photo: © Blaine Harrington III

Distributed to the book trade by
Publishers Group West
Berkeley, California

While every effort has been made to keep the content of this book accurate, the author and publisher accept no responsibility whatsoever for anyone ordering bad beer or getting messed up in any other way because of the linguistic confidence this phrase book has given them.

JMP travel guidebooks by Rick Steves

Europe 101: History and Art for the Traveler (with Gene
   Openshaw)
*Rick Steves' Mona Winks: Self-guided Tours of Europe's Top
   Museums* (with Gene Openshaw)
Rick Steves' Postcards from Europe
Rick Steves' Best of Europe
Rick Steves' Europe Through the Back Door
Rick Steves' France, Belgium & the Netherlands (with Steve
   Smith)
Rick Steves' Germany, Austria & Switzerland
Rick Steves' Great Britain & Ireland
Rick Steves' Italy
Rick Steves' Russia & the Baltics (with Ian Watson)
Rick Steves' Scandinavia
Rick Steves' Spain & Portugal
Rick Steves' London (with Gene Openshaw)
Rick Steves' Paris (with Steve Smith and Gene Openshaw)
Rick Steves' Phrase Books for: French, German, Italian,
   Spanish/Portuguese, and French/Italian/German
Asia Through the Back Door

Rick Steves' company, *Europe Through the Back Door*,
provides many services for budget travelers, including a free
quarterly newsletter/catalog, budget travel books and accessories, Eurailpasses (with free video and travel advice included),
free-spirited European tours, on-line travel tips, and a Travel
Resource Center in Edmonds, WA. For a free newsletter, call,
write, or e-mail:

Europe Through the Back Door
120 Fourth Avenue N., Box 2009
Edmonds, WA 98020 USA
Tel: 425/771-8303, Fax: 425/771-0833
Web: http://www.ricksteves.com
E-mail: rick@ricksteves.com

Contents

Hi, I'm Rick Steves.

I'm the only mono-lingual speaker I know who's had the nerve to design a series of European phrase books. But that's one of the things that makes them better. You see, after 25 summers of travel through Europe, I've learned first-hand (1) what's essential for communication in another country, and (2) what's not. I've assembled these most important words and phrases in a logical, no-frills format, and I've worked with native Europeans and seasoned travelers to give you the simplest, clearest translations possible.

But this book is more than just a pocket translator. The words and phrases have been carefully selected to make you a happier, more effective budget traveler. The key to getting more out of every travel dollar is to get closer to the local people, and to rely less on entertainment, restaurants, and hotels that cater only to foreign tourists. This book will give you the linguistic four-wheel drive to navigate through German, Austrian and Swiss culture—from ordering a meal at a locals-only Tirolean restaurant to discussing social issues, travel dreams, and your *wurst* memories with the family that runs the place. Long after your memories of castles and museums have faded, you'll still treasure the close encounters you had with your new European friends.

A good phrase book should help you enjoy your linguistic adventure—not just survive it—so I've added a healthy dose of humor. But please use these phrases carefully, in a self-effacing spirit. Remember that one ugly American can undo the goodwill built by dozens of culturally-sensitive ones.

To get the most out of this book, take the time to internalize and put into practice my German pronunciation tips. I've spelled out the pronunciations as if you were reading English. Don't worry too much about memorizing grammatical rules, like which gender a particular noun is—toss sex out the window and communicate!

German is the closest thing I'll ever have to a "second language." It takes only a few words to feel like I'm part of the greater Germanic family, greeting hikers in the Alps, commiserating over the crowds in Rothenburg, prosting in the beerhalls of Blindenpist, and slap-dancing in Tirol.

You'll notice that this book has a dictionary and a nifty menu decoder. You'll also find German tongue twisters, international words, telephone tips, and a handy tear-out "cheat sheet." Tear it out and tuck it into your dirndl or lederhosen, so you can easily use it to memorize key phrases during otherwise idle moments. As you prepare for your trip, you may want to take advantage of my annually-updated *Rick Steves' Germany, Austria & Switzerland* guidebook.

My goal is to help you become a more confident, extroverted traveler. If this phrase book helps make that happen, or if you have suggestions for making it better, I'd love to hear from you. I personally read and value all feedback. My address is Europe Through the Back Door, P.O. Box 2009, Edmonds, WA 98020, tel. 425/771-8303, fax 425/771-0833, e-mail: rick@ricksteves.com.

Happy travels, and *Viel Glück* (good luck) as you hurdle the language barrier!

Rick Steves

Getting Started

Versatile, entertaining German

...is spoken throughout Germany, Austria, and most of Switzerland. In addition, German rivals English as the handiest second language in Scandinavia, the Netherlands, Eastern Europe, and Turkey.

German is kind of a "lego language." Be on the lookout for fun combination words. A *Fingerhut* (finger hat) is a thimble, a *Halbinsel* (half island) is a peninsula, a *Stinktier* (stinky animal) is a skunk, and a *Dummkopf* (dumb head) is . . . um . . . uh . . .

German has some key twists to its pronunciation:

CH sounds like the guttural CH in Scottish loch.
J sounds like Y in yes.
S can sound like S in sun or Z in zoo.
   But *S* followed by *CH* sounds like SH in
   shine.
V sounds like F in fun.
W sounds like V in volt.
Z sounds like TS in hits.
EI sounds like I in light.
EU sounds like OY in joy.
IE sounds like EE in seed.

German has a few unusual signs and sounds. The letter *ß* is not a letter B at all—it's the sound of "ss." Some of the German vowels are double-dotted with an "umlaut." The *ü* has a sound uncommon in English. To make the *ü* sound, round your lips to say "o," but say "ee." The German *ch* has a clearing-your-throat sound. Say *Achtung!*

Here's a guide to the phonetics in this book:

ah	like A in father.
ay	like AY in play.
e, eh	like E in let.
ee	like EE in seed.
ehr	sounds like "air."
ew	pucker your lips and say "ee."
g	like G in go.
i	like I in bit.
ī	like I in light.
kh	like the guttural CH in Achtung.
o	like O in cost.
oh	like O in note.
oo	like OO in too.
ow	like OW in cow.
oy	like OY in joy.
ts	like TS in hits. It's a small explosive sound.
u	like U in put.
ur	like UR in purr.

In German, the verb is often at the end of the sentence—it's where the action is. Germans capitalize all nouns. Each noun has a sex which determines which "the" you'll use (*der* man, *die* woman, and *das* neuter). No traveler is expected to remember which is which. It's O.K. to just grab whichever "the" (*der, die, das*) comes to mind. In the interest of simplicity, we've occasionally left out the articles. Also for simplicity, we often drop the "please." Please use "please" (*bitte*) liberally.

Each German-speaking country has a distinct dialect. The Swiss speak a lilting Swiss-German but write High German like the Germans. The multilingual Swiss greet you with a cheery *"Gruetzi,"* use *"Merci"* for thank you, and say goodbye with a *"Ciao."* Both Austrians and Bavarians speak in a sing-song dialect, and greet one another with *"Grüss Gott"* (May God greet you).

German Basics

Meeting and greeting Germans:

Good day.	**Guten Tag.**	**goo**-ten tahg
Good morning.	**Guten Morgen.**	**goo**-ten **mor**-gen
Good evening.	**Guten Abend.**	**goo**-ten ah-bent
Good night.	**Gute Nacht.**	**goo**-teh nahkht
Hi. (informal)	**Hallo.**	**hah**-loh
Welcome!	**Willkommen!**	vil-**kom**-men
Mr. / Ms. /	**Herr / Frau /**	hehr / frow /
Miss (under 18)	**Fräulein**	**froy**-līn
How are you?	**Wie geht's?**	vee gayts
Very well, thanks.	**Sehr gut, danke.**	zehr goot **dahng**-keh
And you?	**Und Ihnen?**	oont **ee**-nen
My name is...	**Ich heiße...**	ikh **hī**-seh
What's your name?	**Wie heißen Sie?**	vee **hī**-sen zee
Pleased to meet you.	**Sehr erfreut.**	zehr ehr-**froyt**
Where are you from?	**Woher kommen Sie?**	**voh**-hehr **kom**-men zee
I am / Are you...?	**Ich bin / Sind Sie...?**	ikh bin / zint zee
...on vacation	**...auf Urlaub**	owf **oor**-lowp
Are you working today?	**Arbeiten Sie heute?**	ar-**bīt**-en zee **hoy**-teh
See you later!	**Bis später!**	bis **shpay**-ter
So long! (informal)	**Tschüss!**	chewss
Goodbye.	**Auf Wiedersehen.**	owf **vee**-der-zayn
Good luck!	**Viel Glück!**	feel glewk
Have a good trip!	**Gute Reise!**	**goo**-teh **rī**-zeh

Survival Phrases

While he used a tank instead of a Eurailpass, General Patton made it all the way to Berlin using only these phrases.

They're repeated on your tear-out "cheat sheet" at the end of this book.

The essentials:

Good day.	**Guten Tag.**	**goo**-ten tahg
Do you speak English?	**Sprechen Sie Englisch?**	**shprekh**-en zee **eng**-lish
Yes. / No.	**Ja. / Nein.**	yah / nīn
I don't speak German.	**Ich spreche kein Deutsch.**	ikh **shprekh**-eh kīn doych
Excuse me.	**Entschuldigung.**	ent-**shool**-dee-goong
I'm sorry.	**Es tut mir leid.**	es toot meer līt
Please.	**Bitte.**	**bit**-teh
Thank you.	**Danke.**	**dahng**-keh
No problem.	**Kein Problem.**	kīn proh-**blaym**
Very good.	**Sehr gut.**	zehr goot
You are very kind.	**Sie sind sehr freundlich.**	zee zint zehr **froynd**-likh
Goodbye.	**Auf Wiedersehen.**	owf **vee**-der-zayn

Where?

Where is...?	**Wo ist...?**	voh ist
...a hotel	**...ein Hotel**	īn hoh-**tel**
...a youth hostel	**...eine Jugend- herberge**	ī-neh **yoo**-gend- hehr-behr-geh
...a restaurant	**...ein Restaurant**	īn res-tow-**rahnt**
...a supermarket	**...ein Supermarkt**	īn **zoo**-per-markt
...a pharmacy	**...eine Apotheke**	ī-neh ah-poh-**tay**-keh

...a bank	...eine Bank	ī-neh bahnk
...the train station	...der Bahnhof	dehr **bahn**-hohf
...the tourist information office	...das Touristen-informationsbüro	dahs **too**-ris-ten-in-for-**maht**-see-ohns-**bew**-roh
...the toilet	...die Toilette	dee toh-**leh**-teh
men / women	Herren / Damen	**hehr**-ren / **dah**-men

How much?

How much is it?	Wieviel kostet das?	vee-**feel kos**-tet dahs
Write it?	Schreiben?	**shrī**-ben
Cheap / Cheaper / Cheapest.	Billig / Billiger / Am Billigsten.	**bil**-lig / **bil**-lig-er / ahm **bil**-lig-sten
Is it free?	Ist es umsonst?	ist es oom-**zohnst**
Included?	Inklusive?	in-**kloo**-sev
Do you have...?	Haben Sie...?	**hah**-ben zee
Where can I buy...?	Wo kann ich kaufen...?	voh kahn ikh **kow**-fen
I would like...	Ich hätte gern...	ikh **het**-teh gehrn
We would like...	Wir hätten gern...	veer **het**-ten gehrn
...this.	...dies.	deez
...just a little.	...nur ein bißchen.	noor īn **bis**-yen
...more.	...mehr.	mehr
...a ticket.	...eine Karte.	ī-neh **kar**-teh
...a room.	...ein Zimmer.	īn **tsim**-mer
...the bill.	...die Rechnung.	dee **rekh**-noong

How many?

one	eins	īns
two	zwei	tsvī
three	drei	drī
four	vier	feer
five	fünf	fewnf
six	sechs	zex
seven	sieben	zee-ben
eight	acht	ahkht
nine	neun	noyn
ten	zehn	tsayn

You'll find more to count on in the Numbers chapter.

When?

At what time?	Um wieviel Uhr?	oom vee-feel oor
Just a moment.	Moment.	moh-ment
now / soon / later	jetzt / bald / später	yetzt / bahld / shpay-ter
today / tomorrow	heute / morgen	hoy-teh / mor-gen

Be creative! You can combine these survival phrases to say: "Two, please," or "No, thank you," or "I'd like a cheap hotel," or "Cheaper, please?" Please is a magic word in any language. If you want something and you don't know the word for it, just point and say, *"Bitte"* (Please). If you know the word for what you want, such as the bill, simply say, *"Rechnung, bitte"* (Bill, please).

Struggling with German:

Do you speak English?	**Sprechen Sie Englisch?**	**shprekh**-en zee **eng**-lish
A teeny weeny bit?	**Ein ganz klein bißchen?**	īn gahnts klīn **bis**-yen
Please speak English.	**Bitte sprechen Sie Englisch.**	**bit**-teh **shprekh**-en zee **eng**-lish
You speak English well.	**Ihr Englisch ist sehr gut.**	eer **eng**-lish ist zehr goot
I don't speak German.	**Ich spreche kein Deutsch.**	ikh **shprekh**-eh kīn doych
I speak a little German.	**Ich spreche ein bißchen Deutsch.**	ikh **shprekh**-eh īn **bis**-yən doych
What is this in German?	**Wie heißt das auf Deutsch?**	vee hīst dahs owf doych
Repeat?	**Noch einmal?**	nokh **īn**-mahl
Please speak slowly.	**Bitte sprechen Sie langsam.**	**bit**-teh **shprekh**-en zee **lahng**-zahm
Slower.	**Langsamer.**	**lahng**-zah-mer
I understand.	**Ich verstehe.**	ikh fehr-**shtay**-heh
I don't understand.	**Ich verstehe nicht.**	ikh fehr-**shtay**-heh nikht
Do you understand?	**Verstehen Sie?**	fehr-**shtay**-hen zee
Write it?	**Schreiben?**	shrī-ben
Does someone there speak English?	**Spricht dort jemand Englisch?**	shprikt dort **yay**-mahnt **eng**-lish
Who speaks English?	**Wer kann Englisch?**	vehr kahn **eng**-lish

Handy questions:

How much?	**Wieviel?**	vee-**feel**
How many?	**Wieviele?**	vee-**fee**-leh
How long...?	**Wie lang...?**	vee lahng
...is the trip	**...dauert die Reise**	**dow**-ert dee **rī**-zeh
How many minutes?	**Wieviele Minuten?**	vee-**fee**-leh mee-**noo**-ten
How many hours?	**Wieviele Stunden?**	vee-**fee**-leh **shtoon**-den
How far?	**Wie weit?**	vee vīt
How?	**Wie?**	vee
Is it possible?	**Ist es möglich?**	ist es **mur**-glikh
Is it necessary?	**Ist das nötig?**	ist dahs **nur**-tig
Can you help me?	**Können Sie mir helfen?**	**kurn**-nen zee meer **hehl**-fen
What? (didn't hear)	**Wie bitte?**	vee **bit**-teh
What is that?	**Was ist das?**	vahs ist dahs
What is better?	**Was ist besser?**	vahs ist **bes**-ser
What's going on?	**Was ist los?**	vahs ist lohs
When?	**Wann?**	vahn
What time is it?	**Wie spät ist es?**	vee shpayt ist es
At what time?	**Um wieviel Uhr?**	oom vee-**feel** oor
On time? Late?	**Pünktlich? Spät?**	**pewnkt**-likh / shpayt
When does this...?	**Um wieviel Uhr ist hier...?**	oom vee-**feel** oor ist heer
...open	**...geöffnet**	geh-**urf**-net
...close	**...geschlossen**	geh-**shlos**-sen
Where is / are...?	**Wo ist / sind...?**	voh ist / zint
Where can I find / buy...?	**Wo kann ich... finden / kaufen?**	voh kahn ikh... **fin**-den / **kow**-fen

BASICS

Do you have...?	Haben Sie...?	**hah**-ben zee
Anything else?	Sonst noch etwas?	zohnst nokh **et**-vahs
Can I...?	Kann ich...?	kahn ikh
Can we...?	Können wir...?	**kurn**-nen veer
...have one	...eins haben	īns **hah**-ben
...go free	...unsonst rein	oom-**zohnst** rīn
Who?	Wer?	vehr
Why?	Warum?	vah-**room**
Why not?	Warum nicht?	vah-**room** nikht
Yes or no?	Ja oder nein?	yah **oh**-der nīn

To prompt a simple answer, ask, *"Ja oder nein?"* (Yes or no?). To turn a word or sentence into a question, ask it in a questioning tone. An easy way to ask, "Where is the toilet?" is to say, *"Toilette?"*

Das yin und yang:

cheap / expensive	billig / teuer	**bil**-lig / **toy**-er
big / small	groß / klein	grohs / klīn
hot / cold	heiß / kalt	hīs / kahlt
open / closed	geöffnet / geschlossen	geh-**urf**-net / geh-**shlos**-sen
entrance / exit	Eingang / Ausgang	**īn**-gahng / **ows**-gahng
push / pull	drücken / ziehen	**drewk**-en / **tsee**-hen
arrive / depart	ankommen / abfahren	**ahn**-kom-men / **ahp**-fah-ren
early / late	früh / spät	frew / shpayt
soon / later	bald / später	bahld / **shpay**-ter
fast / slow	schnell / langsam	shnel / **lahng**-zahm

here / there	**hier / dort**	heer / dort
near / far	**nah / fern**	nah / fehrn
indoors / outdoors	**drinnen / draussen**	**drin**-nen / **drow**-sen
good / bad	**gut / schlecht**	goot / shlekht
best / worst	**beste / schlechteste**	**bes**-teh / **shlekh**-tes-teh
a little / lots	**wenig / viel**	**vay**-nig / feel
more / less	**mehr / weniger**	mehr / **vay**-nig-er
mine / yours	**mein / ihr**	mīn / eer
everybody / nobody	**jeder / keiner**	**yay**-der / **kī**-ner
easy / difficult	**leicht / schwierig**	līkht / **shvee**-rig
left / right	**links / rechts**	links / rekhts
up / down	**oben / unten**	**oh**-ben / **oon**-ten
above / below	**obere / untere**	**oh**-ber-eh / **oon**-ter-eh
young / old	**jung / alt**	yoong / ahlt
new / old	**neu / alt**	noy / ahlt
heavy / light	**schwer / leicht**	shvehr / līkht
dark / light	**dunkel / hell**	**dun**-kel / hel
happy / sad	**glücklich / traurig**	**glewk**-likh / **trow**-rig
beautiful / ugly	**schön / häßlich**	shurn / **hes**-likh
nice / mean	**nett / gemein**	net / geh-**mīn**
smart / stupid	**klug / dumm**	kloog / dum
vacant / occupied	**frei / besetzt**	frī / beh-**zetst**
with / without	**mit / ohne**	mit / **oh**-neh

Big little words:

I	**ich**	ikh
you (formal)	**Sie**	zee
you (informal)	**du**	doo
we	**wir**	veer

he	**er**	ehr
she	**sie**	zee
they	**sie**	zee
and	**und**	oont
at	**bei**	bī
because	**weil**	vīl
but	**aber**	**ah**-ber
by (via)	**mit**	mit
for	**für**	fewr
from	**von**	fon
here	**hier**	heer
if	**ob**	ohp
in	**in**	in
not	**nicht**	nikht
now	**jetzt**	yetst
only	**nur**	noor
or	**oder**	**oh**-der
this / that	**dies / das**	deez / dahs
to	**nach**	nahkh
very	**sehr**	zehr

Das Alphabet:

In case you need to spell your name out loud or participate in a spelling bee:

a	ah	**j**	yot	**s**	"s"
ä	ay	**k**	kah	**t**	tay
b	bay	**l**	"l"	**u**	oo
c	tsay	**m**	"m"	**ü**	ew
d	day	**n**	"n"	**v**	fow
e	ay	**o**	"o"	**w**	vay
f	"f"	**ö**	ur	**x**	eeks
g	gay	**p**	pay	**y**	ewp-sil-lon
h	hah	**q**	koo	**z**	tseht
i	ee	**r**	ehr	**ß**	"s"

Very German expressions:

Ach so.	ahkh zoh	I see.
Achtung.	ahkh-toong	Attention.
Alles klar.	**ah**-les klar	Everything is clear.
Ausgezeichnet.	ows-get-**tsīkh**-net	Excellent.
Bitte.	**bit**-teh	Please. / You're welcome. Can I help you?
Es geht.	es gayt	So-so.
Gemütlich.	geh-**mewt**-likh	Cozy. (see note below)
Genau.	geh-**now**	Exactly.
Halt.	hahlt	Stop.
Kein Wunder.	kīn **voon**-dehr	No wonder.
Mach schnell!	mahkh shnel	Hurry up!
Natürlich.	**nah**-tewr-likh	Naturally.
Prima.	**pree**-mah	Great.
Stimmt.	shtimt	Correct.

Gemütlich (the adjective) and *Gemütlichkeit* (the noun) refer to a special Bavarian or Tirolian coziness. A candle-lit dinner, a friendly pub, a strolling violinist under a grape arbor on a balmy evening...this is *gemütlich*.

German names for places:

Germany	**Deutschland**	**doych**-lahnd
Munich	**München**	**mewnkh**-en
Bavaria	**Bayern**	**bī**-ehrn
Black Forest	**Schwarzwald**	**shvartz**-vahld
Danube	**Donau**	**doh**-now

BASICS

Austria	Österreich	urs-tehr-rīkh
Vienna	Wien	veen
Switzerland	Schweiz	shvīts
Italy	Italien	i-tah-lee-en
Venice	Venedig	veh-neh-dig
France	Frankreich	frahnk-rīkh
Spain	Spanien	shpahn-ee-en
Netherlands	Niederlande	nee-der-lahn-deh
England	England	eng-glahnd
Greece	Griechenland	greekh-en-lahnd
Turkey	Türkei	tewr-kī
Europe	Europa	oy-roh-pah
United Europe	Vereinigtes Europa	fehr-ī-nig-tehs oy-roh-pah
Russia	Rußland	roos-lahnd
Africa	Afrika	ah-free-kah
United States	U.S.A.	oo ehs ah
Canada	Kanada	kah-nah-dah
world	Welt	velt

If you're using *Rick Steves' Germany, Austria & Switzerland* guidebook, here are a few more place names:

Bacharach (Ger.)	bahkh-ah-rahkh
Jungfrau (Switz.)	yoong-frow
Kleine Scheidegg (Switz.)	klī-neh shī-deg
Köln (Ger.)	kurln
Mosel (Ger.)	moh-zehl
Neuschwanstein (Ger.)	noysh-vahn-shtīn
Reutte (Aus.)	roy-teh
Rothenburg (Ger.)	roh-ten-berg

Numbers

0	null	nool
1	eins	īns
2	zwei	tsvī
3	drei	drī
4	vier	feer
5	fünf	fewnf
6	sechs	zex
7	sieben	zee-ben
8	acht	ahkht
9	neun	noyn
10	zehn	tsayn
11	elf	elf
12	zwölf	tsvurlf
13	dreizehn	drī-tsayn
14	vierzehn	feer-tsayn
15	fünfzehn	fewnf-tsayn
16	sechzehn	zekh-tsayn
17	siebzehn	zeeb-tsayn
18	achtzehn	ahkht-tsayn
19	neunzehn	noyn-tsayn
20	zwanzig	tsvahn-tsig
21	einundzwanzig	īn-oont-tsvahn-tsig
22	zweiundzwanzig	tsvī-oont-tsvahn-tsig
23	dreiundzwanzig	drī-oont-tsvahn-tsig
30	dreißig	drī-sig
31	einunddreißig	īn-oont-drī-sig
40	vierzig	feer-tsig
41	einundvierzig	īn-oont-feer-tsig
50	fünfzig	fewnf-tsig

60	**sechzig**	**zekh**-tsig
70	**siebzig**	**zeeb**-tsig
80	**achtzig**	**ahkht**-tsig
90	**neunzig**	**noyn**-tsig
100	**hundert**	**hoon**-dert
101	**hunderteins**	hoon-dert-**īns**
102	**hundertzwei**	hoon-dert-**tsvī**
200	**zweihundert**	**tsvī**-hoon-dert
1000	**tausend**	**tow**-zend
2000	**zweitausend**	**tsvī**-tow-zend
2001	**zweitausendeins**	**tsvī**-tow-zend-**īns**
10,000	**zehntausend**	**tsayn**-tow-zend
million	**eine Million**	**ī**-neh mil-**yohn**
billion	**eine Milliarde**	**ī**-neh mil-**yar**-deh
first	**erste**	**ehr**-steh
second	**zweite**	**tsvī**-teh
third	**dritte**	**drit**-teh
half	**halb**	hahlp
100%	**hundert Prozent**	**hoon**-dert proh-**tsent**
number one	**Nummer eins**	**num**-mer īns

The number *zwei* (two) is sometimes pronounced "zwoh" to help distinguish it from the similar sound of *eins* (one).

Remember the nursery rhyme about the four-and-twenty blackbirds? That's how Germans say the numbers from 21 to 99 (e.g., 59 = neunundfünfzig = nine-and-fifty).

Money

Can you change dollars?	Können Sie Dollar wechseln?	**kurn**-nen zee **dol**-lar **vekh**-seln
What is your exchange rate for dollars...?	Was ist ihr Wechselkurs für Dollars...?	vahs ist eer **vekh**-sel-koors fewr **dol**-lars
...in traveler's checks	...in Reiseschecks	in **rī**-zeh-sheks
What is the commission?	Wieviel ist die Kommission?	vee-**feel** ist dee kom-mis-see-**ohn**
Any extra fee?	Extra Gebühren?	**ex**-trah geh-**bew**-ren
I would like...	Ich hätte gern...	ikh **het**-teh gehrn
...small bills.	...kleine Banknoten.	**klī**-neh **bahnk**-noh-ten
...large bills.	...große Banknoten.	**groh**-seh **bahnk**-noh-ten
...coins.	...Münzen.	**mewn**-tsen
...small change.	...Kleingeld.	**klīn**-gelt
Is this a mistake?	Ist das ein Fehler?	ist dahs īn **fay**-lehr
I'm...	Ich bin...	ikh bin
...broke / poor / rich.	...pleite / arm / reich.	**plī**-teh / arm / **rīkh**
55 DM	fünfundfünfzig Mark	fewnf-oont-**fewnf**-tsig mark
50 Pf	fünfzig Pfennig	**fewnf**-tsig **fehn**-nig
euro	Euro	**yoo**-roh
Where is a cash machine?	Wo ist der Bankomat?	voh ist dehr **bahnk**-oh-maht

When using a *Bankomat* (ATM machine), you'll see these three buttons: *Abbruch* (cancel), *Korrektour* (change or correct), and *Bestätigung* (affirm). Your PIN number is a *Geheimnummer*.

Key money words:

bank	**Bank**	**bahnk**
cash machine	**Bankomat**	**bahnk**-oh-maht
money	**Geld**	gelt
change money	**Geld wechseln**	gelt **vekh**-seln
exchange	**Wechsel**	**vekh**-sel
buy / sell	**kaufen / verkaufen**	**kow**-fen / **fehr**-kow-fen
commission	**Kommission**	kom-mis-see-**ohn**
traveler's check	**Reisescheck**	**rī**-zeh-shek
credit card	**Kreditkarte**	kreh-**deet**-kar-teh
cash advance	**Vorschuß in Bargeld**	**for**-shoos in **bar**-gelt
cashier	**Kassierer**	kah-**seer**-er
cash	**Bargeld**	**bar**-gelt
bills	**Banknoten**	**bahnk**-noh-ten
coins	**Münzen**	**mewn**-tsen
receipt	**Beleg**	bay-**leg**

German marks (DM) are divided into 100 pfennigs (Pf). Swiss francs (Fr) are divided into 100 centimes (c) or rappen (Rp). Use your common cents—pfennigs and centimes are like pennies, and each country has coins like nickels, dimes, and quarters. Austrian schillings are divided into 100 groschen, but since one schilling (1 AS) is worth about a dime, you'll rarely see coins less than a schilling.

None of this will matter after 2002 when the common currency throughout Europe's 11-country Euroland will be the Euro (€).

Time

What time is it?	**Wie spät ist es?**	vee shpayt ist es
It's...	**Es ist...**	es ist
...8:00.	**...acht Uhr.**	ahkht oor
...16:00.	**...sechzehn Uhr.**	**zekh**-tsayn oor
...4:00 in the afternoon.	**...vier Uhr nachmittags.**	feer oor **nahkh**-mit-tahgs
...10:30 (half eleven) in the evening.	**...halb elf Uhr abends.**	hahlp elf oor **ah**-bents
...a quarter past nine.	**...viertel nach neun.**	**feer**-tel nahkh noyn
...a quarter to eleven.	**...viertel vor elf.**	**feer**-tel for elf
...noon.	**...Mittag.**	**mit**-tahg
...midnight.	**...Mitternacht.**	**mit**-ter-nahkht
...sunrise.	**...Sonnenaufgang.**	**zoh**-nen-owf-gahng
...sunset.	**...Sonnenuntergang.**	**zoh**-nen-oon-ter-gahng
...early / late.	**...früh / spät.**	frew / shpayt
...on time.	**...pünktlich.**	**pewnkt**-likh

In Germany, the 24-hour clock (or military time) is used by hotels, for the opening and closing hours of museums, and for train, bus, and boat schedules. Informally, the Germans use the same "12-hour clock" we use.

People use the greeting *"Guten Morgen"* (Good morning) until noon, and *"Guten Tag"* (Good day) switches to *"Guten Abend"* (Good evening) around 6 p.m.

Timely words:

minute	**Minute**	mee-**noo**-teh
hour	**Stunde**	**shtoon**-deh
morning	**Morgen**	**mor**-gen
afternoon	**Nachmittag**	**nahkh**-mit-tahg
evening	**Abend**	**ah**-bent
night	**Nacht**	nahkht
day	**Tag**	tahg
today	**heute**	**hoy**-teh
yesterday	**gestern**	**geh**-stern
tomorrow	**morgen**	**mor**-gen
tomorow morning	**morgen früh**	**mor**-gen frew
anytime	**jederzeit**	yay-der-**tsīt**
immediately	**jetzt**	yetst
in one hour	**in einer Stunde**	in ī-ner **shtoon**-deh
every hour	**jede Stunde**	**yay**-deh **shtoon**-deh
every day	**jeden Tag**	**yay**-den tahg
last	**letzte**	**lehts**-teh
this	**diese**	**dee**-zeh
next	**nächste**	**nekh**-steh
May 15	**fünfzehnten Mai**	**fewnf**-tsayn-ten mī
high season	**Hochsaison**	**hokh**-say-zohn
low season	**Nebensaison**	**nee**-ben-say-zohn
in the future	**in Zukunft**	in tsoo-koonft
in the past	**in der Vergangenheit**	in dehr fehr-**gahng**-en-hīt

For dates of the month, take any number, add the sound "ten" to the end, then say the month. June 19 is *neunzehnten Juni.*

week	**Woche**	**vokh**-eh
Monday	**Montag**	**mohn**-tahg
Tuesday	**Dienstag**	**deen**-stahg
Wednesday	**Mittwoch**	**mit**-vokh
Thursday	**Donnerstag**	**don**-ner-stahg
Friday	**Freitag**	**frī**-tahg
Saturday	**Samstag, Sonnabend**	**zahm**-stahg, **zon**-ah-bent
Sunday	**Sonntag**	**zon**-tahg
month	**Monat**	**moh**-naht
January	**Januar**	**yah**-noo-ar
February	**Februar**	**fay**-broo-ar
March	**März**	mehrts
April	**April**	ah-**pril**
May	**Mai**	mī
June	**Juni**	**yoo**-nee
July	**Juli**	**yoo**-lee
August	**August**	**ow**-gust
September	**September**	sep-**tem**-ber
October	**Oktober**	ok-**toh**-ber
November	**November**	noh-**vem**-ber
December	**Dezember**	day-**tsem**-ber
year	**Jahr**	yar
spring	**Frühling**	**frew**-ling
summer	**Sommer**	**zom**-mer
fall	**Herbst**	hehrpst
winter	**Winter**	**vin**-ter

TIME

Happy days and holidays:

holiday	**Feiertag**	**fī**-er-tahg
national holiday	**staatlicher Feiertag**	**shtaht**-likh-er **fī**-er-tahg
religious holiday	**religiöser Feiertag**	reh-lig-ee-**ur**-zer **fī**-er-tahg
Is today / tomorrow a holiday?	**Ist heute / morgen ein Feiertag?**	ist **hoy**-teh / **mor**-gen īn **fī**-er-tahg
What is the holiday?	**Welcher Feiertag ist das?**	**velkh**-er **fī**-er-tahg dahs
Easter	**Ostern**	**ohs**-tern
Merry Christmas!	**Fröhliche Weihnachten!**	**frur**-likh-eh **vī**-nahkh-ten
Happy new year!	**Glückliches Neues Jahr!**	**glewk**-likh-es **noy**-es yar
Happy anniversary!	**Herzlichen Glückwunsch!**	**hehrts**-likh-en **glewk**-vunch
Happy birthday!	**Herzlichen Glückwunsch zum Geburtstag!**	**hehrts**-likh-en **glewk**-vunch tsoom geh-**boort**-stahg

Germans sing "Happy birthday" to the tune we use, sometimes even in English. The German version means "On your birthday, best wishes": *Zum Geburtstag, viel Glück, Zum Geburtstag, viel Glück, Zum Geburtstag, liebe ___, Zum Geburtstag, viel Glück.*

Other German celebrations include *Karneval* (or *Fasching*), a week-long festival of parades and partying. It happens before Lent in February, and *Köln* is the center of the revelry. *Christi Himmelfahrt*, or the Ascension of Christ, comes in May, and doubles for Father's Day. You'll see men in groups on pilgrimages through the countryside, usually carrying beer or heading towards it.

Germany's national holiday is Oct. 3, Austria's is Oct. 26, and Switzerland's is Aug. 1.

TIME

Transportation

Trains:

Is this the line for...?	**Ist das die Schlange für...?**	ist dahs dee **shlahn**-geh fewr
...tickets	**...Fahrkarten**	**far**-kar-ten
...reservations	**...Reservierungen**	reh-zehr-**feer**-oon-gen
How much is a ticket to...?	**Wieviel kostet eine Fahrkarte nach...?**	vee-**feel kos**-tet ī-neh **far**-kar-teh nahkh
A ticket to ___.	**Eine Fahrkarte nach ___.**	ī-neh **far**-kar-teh nahkh
When is the next train?	**Wann ist der nächste Zug?**	vahn ist dehr **nekh**-steh tsoog
I'd like to leave...	**Ich möchte... abfahren.**	ikh **murkh**-teh... **ahp**-fah-ren
I'd like to arrive...	**Ich möchte... ankommen.**	ikh **murkh**-teh... **ahn**-kom-men
...by ___.	**...vor ___**	for
...in the morning.	**...am Morgen**	ahm **mor**-gen
...in the afternoon.	**...am Nachmittag**	ahm **nahkh**-mit-tahg
...in the evening.	**...am Abend**	ahm **ah**-bent
Is there a...?	**Gibt es einen...?**	gipt es ī-nen
...earlier train	**...früherer Zug**	**frew**-hehr-er tsoog

...later train	...späterer Zug	shpay-ter-er tsoog
...overnight train	...Nachtzug	nahkht-tsoog
...supplement	...Zuschlag	tsoo-shlahg
Does my railpass cover the supplement?	Ist der Zuschlag in meinem Railpass enthalten?	ist dehr tsoosh-lahg in mi-nem rayl-pahs ent-hahl-ten
Is there a discount for...?	Gibt es Ermäßigung für...?	gipt es ehr-may-see-goong fewr
...youths	...Jugendliche	yoo-gend-likh-eh
...seniors	...Senioren	zen-yor-en
Is a reservation required?	Brauche ich eine Platzkarte?	browkh-eh ikh i-neh plahts-kar-teh
I'd like to reserve a...	Ich möchte einen... reservieren.	ikh murkh-teh i-nen... reh-zer-vee-ren
...seat.	...Sitzplatz	zits-plahts
...berth.	...Liegewagenplatz	lee-geh-vah-gen-plahts
...sleeper.	...Schlafwagenplatz	shlahf-vah-gen-plahts
Where does the train leave from?	Wo fährt er der Zug ab?	voh fayrt ehr dehr tsoog ahp
What track?	Welches Gleis?	velkh-es glis
On time? Late?	Pünktlich? Spät?	pewnkt-likh / shpayt
When will it arrive?	Wann kommt er an?	vahn komt ehr ahn
Is it direct?	Direktverbindung?	dee-rekt-fehr-bin-doong
Must I transfer?	Muß ich umsteigen?	mus ikh oom-shti-gen
When? Where?	Wann? Wo?	vahn / voh
Which train to...?	Welcher Zug nach...?	velkh-er tsoog nahkh
Which train car to...?	Welcher Wagen nach...?	velkh-er vah-gen nahkh
Where is first class?	Wo ist die erste Klasse?	voh ist dee ehr-steh klah-seh

TRANSPORTATION

...front / middle / back	...vorne / mitte / hinten	for-neh / mit-teh / hin-ten
Is this seat free?	Ist dieser Platz frei?	ist dee-zer plahts frī
That's my seat.	Das ist mein Platz.	dahs ist mīn plahts
Save my place?	Halten Sie meinen Platz frei?	hahl-ten zee mī-nen plahts frī
Where are you going?	Wohin fahren Sie?	voh-hin far-en zee
I'm going to...	Ich fahre nach...	ikh far-reh nahkh
Can you tell me when to get off?	Können Sie mir Bescheid sagen?	kurn-nen zee meer beh-shīt zah-gen
Is there a train to / from the airport?	Gibt es einen Zug zum / vom Flughafen?	gipt es ī-nen tsoog tsoom / fom floog-hah-fen

Ticket talk:

ticket window	Fahrscheine	far-shī-neh
reservations window	Reservierungen	reh-zehr-feer-oon-gen
national / international	Inland / Ausland	in-lahnt / ows-lahnt
ticket	Fahrkarte	far-kar-teh
one-way ticket	Hinfahrkarte	hin-far-kar-teh
roundtrip ticket	Rückfahrkarte	rewk-far-kar-teh
first class	erste Klasse	ehr-steh klah-seh
second class	zweite Klasse	tsvī-teh klah-seh
non-smoking	Nichtraucher	nikht-rowkh-er
reduced fare	verbilligte Karte	fehr-bil-lig-teh kar-teh
validate	abstempeln	ahp-shtem-peln
schedule	Fahrplan	far-plahn
departure	Abfahrtszeit	ahp-farts-tsīt
direct	Direkt	dee-rekt

transfer	Umsteigen	**oom**-shtī-gen
connection	Anschluß	**ahn**-shlus
with supplement	mit Zuschlag	mit **tsoosh**-lahg
reservation	Platzkarte	**plahts**-kar-teh
seat	Platz	plahts
window seat	Fensterplatz	**fen**-ster-plahts
aisle seat	Platz am Gang	plahts ahm gahng
berth...	Liege...	**lee**-geh
...upper	...obere	**oh**-ber-eh
...middle	...mittlere	mit-**leh**-reh
...lower	...untere	**oon**-ter-eh
refund	Rückvergütung	**rewk**-fehr-gew-toong

At the train station:

German Railways	Deutsche Bundes-bahn (DB)	**doy**-cheh **boon**-des-bahn (day bay)
train station	Bahnhof	**bahn**-hohf
central train station	Hauptbahnhof	**howpt**-bahn-hohf
train information	Zugauskunft	tsoog-**ows**-koonft
train	Zug, Eisenbahn	tsoog, **ī**-zen-bahn
fast train	Intercity, Schnellzug	"inter-city," **shnel**-tsoog
fastest train	ICE	ee tsay ay
arrival	Ankunft	**ahn**-koonft
departure	Abfahrt	**ahp**-fart
delay	Verspätung	fehr-**shpay**-toong
toilet	Toilette	toh-**leh**-teh
waiting room	Wartesaal	**var**-teh-zahl
lockers	Schließfächer	**shlees**-fekh-er
baggage check room	Gepäckaufgabe	geh-**pek**-owf-**gah**-beh

lost and found office	**Fundbüro**	**foond**-bew-roh
tourist information	**Touristen-information**	**too**-ris-ten-in-for-maht-see-**ohn**
to the trains	**zu den Zugen**	tsoo dayn **tsoo**-gen
platform	**Bahnsteig**	**bahn**-shtīg
track	**Gleis**	glīs
train car	**Wagen**	**vah**-gen
dining car	**Speisewagen**	shpī-zeh-**vah**-gen
sleeper car	**Liegewagen**	**lee**-geh-**vah**-gen
conductor	**Schaffner**	**shahf**-ner

As you approach a station you will hear an announcement such as: *In wenigen minuten erreichen wir in München.* (In a few minutes, we will arrive in Munich.)

German schedules use the 24-hour clock. It's like American time until noon. After that, subtract twelve and add p.m. So 13:00 is 1 p.m., 20:00 is 8 p.m., and 24:00 is midnight. One minute after midnight is 00:01.

Reading train schedules:

Abfahrt	departure
Ankunft	arrival
auch	also
außer	except
bis	until
Feiertag	holiday
gleis	track
jeden	every
nach	to
nicht	not
nur	only
Richtung	direction

Samstag	Saturday
Sonntag	Sunday
täglich (tgl.)	daily
tagsüber	days
über	via
verspätet	late
von	from
werktags	Monday-Saturday (workdays)
wochentags	weekdays
zeit	time
ziel	destination
1-5, 6, 7	Monday-Friday, Saturday, Sunday

TRANSPORTATION

Major rail lines in Germany

Buses and subways:

How do I get to...?	**Wie komme ich zu...?**	vee **kom**-meh ikh tsoo
Which bus to...?	**Welcher Bus nach...?**	**velkh**-er boos nahkh
Does it stop at...?	**Hält er in...?**	helt er in
Which stop for...?	**Welche Haltestelle für...?**	**velkh**-eh **hahl**-teh-shtel-leh fewr
Which direction for...?	**Welche Richtung nach...?**	**velkh**-eh **rikh**-toong nahkh
Must I transfer?	**Muß ich umsteigen?**	mus ikh **oom**-shtī-gen
How much is a ticket?	**Wieviel kostet eine Fahrkarte?**	vee-**feel** kos-tet ī-neh **far**-kar-teh
Where can I buy a ticket?	**Wo kaufe ich eine Fahrkarte?**	voh **kow**-feh ikh ī-neh **far**-kar-teh
Is there a...?	**Gibt es eine...?**	gipt es ī-neh
...one-day pass	**...Tageskarte**	**tahg**-es-kar-teh
...discount for buying more tickets	**...Preisnachlaß, wenn ich mehrere Fahrkarten kaufe?**	prīs-**nahkh**-lahs ven ikh **meh**-reh-reh **far**-kar-ten **kow**-feh
When is the...?	**Wann fährt der... ab?**	vahn fart dehr... ahp
...first	**...erste**	**ehr**-steh
...next	**...nächste**	**nekh**-steh
...last	**...letzte**	**lets**-teh
...bus / subway	**...Bus / U-Bahn**	boos / **oo**-bahn
What's the frequency per hour / day?	**Wie oft pro Stunde / Tag?**	vee oft proh **shtoon**-deh / tahg
I'm going to...	**Ich fahre nach...**	ikh **far**-eh nahkh
Can you tell me when to get off?	**Können Sie mir Bescheid sagen?**	**kurn**-nen zee meer beh-**shīt** zah-gen

Is there a bus to / from the airport?	**Gibt es einen Bus zum / vom Flughafen?**	gipt es ī-nen boos tsoom / fom **floog**-hah-fen

Key bus & subway words:

ticket	**Fahrkarte**	**far**-kar-teh
short-ride ticket	**Kurzstrecke**	**koorts**-strekh-keh
day ticket	**Tageskarte**	**tahg**-es-kar-teh
one-ride ticket	**Einzelfahrkarte**	**īn**-tsel-far-**kar**-teh
strip card	**Streifenkarte**	**shtrī**-fen-kar-teh
fare	**Betrag**	beh-**trahg**
bus	**Bus**	boos
bus stop	**Bushaltestelle**	**boos**-hahl-teh-**shtel**-leh
bus station	**Busbahnhof**	**boos**-bahn-hof
subway	**U-Bahn**	**oo**-bahn
subway map	**U-Bahnstrechenplan**	**oo**-bahn-**shtrekh**-en-plahn
subway entrance	**U-Bahneingang**	**oo**-bahn-**īn**-gahng
subway stop	**U-Bahnhaltestelle**	**oo**-bahn-hahl-teh-**shtel**-leh
subway exit	**U-Bahnausgang**	**oo**-bahn-ows-gahng
direct	**Direkt**	dee-**rekt**
direction	**Richtung**	**rikh**-toong
connection	**Anschluß**	**ahn**-shlus
pickpocket	**Taschendieb**	**tahsh**-en-deep

Most big cities offer deals on transportation, such as one-day tickets, cheaper fares for youths and seniors, or a discount for buying a batch of tickets (which you can share with friends). Major cities in Germany, such as Munich and Berlin, have a *U-Bahn* (subway) and *S-Bahn* (urban rail system). If your Eurailpass is valid on the day you're traveling, you can use the *S-Bahn* for free. On a map, *Standort* means "you are here."

Taxis:

Taxi!	**Taxi!**	**tahk**-see
Can you call a taxi?	**Können Sie mir ein Taxi rufen?**	**kurn**-nen zee meer īn **tahk**-see **roo**-fen
Where is a taxi stand?	**Wo ist ein Taxistand?**	voh ist īn **tahk**-see-shtahnt
Are you free?	**Sind Sie frei?**	zint zee frī
Occupied.	**Besetzt.**	beh-**zetst**
How much will it cost to...?	**Wieviel kostet die Fahrt...?**	vee-**feel kos**-tet dee fart
...the airport	**...zum Flughafen**	zoom **floog**-hah-fen
...the train station	**...zum Bahnhof**	zoom **bahn**-hof
...this address	**...zu dieser Adresse**	zoo **dee**-zer ah-**dres**-seh
Too much.	**Zu viel.**	tsoo feel
This is all I have.	**Mehr habe ich nicht.**	mehr **hah**-beh ikh nikht
Can you take ___ people?	**Können Sie ___ Personen mitnehman?**	**kurn**-nen zee ___ pehr-**zoh**-nen mit-**nay**-mahn
Any extra fee?	**Extra Gebühren?**	**ex**-trah geh-**bew**-ren
The meter, please.	**Den Zähler, bitte.**	dayn **tsay**-ler **bit**-teh
Where is the meter?	**Wo ist der Zähler?**	voh ist dehr **tsay**-ler
The most direct route.	**Auf direktem Weg.**	owf dee-**rek**-tem vayg
I'm in a hurry.	**Ich habe wenig Zeit.**	ikh **hah**-beh **vay**-nig tsīt
Slow down.	**Fahren Sie langsamer.**	**far**-en zee **lahng**-zah-mer

If you don't slow down, I'll throw up.	Wenn Sie nicht langsamer fahren, muss ich kotzen.	ven zee nikht **lahng**-zah-mer **far**-en moos ikh **koht**-tsen
Stop here.	Halten Sie hier.	**hahl**-ten zee heer
Can you wait?	Können Sie warten?	**kurn**-nen zee **var**-ten
I'll never forget this ride.	Diese Fahrt werde ich nie vergessen.	**dee**-zeh fart **vehr**-deh ikh nee fehr-**geh**-sen
Where did you learn to drive?	Wo haben Sie Autofahren gelernt?	voh **hah**-ben zee **ow**-toh-far-en geh-**lehrnt**
I'll only pay what's on the meter.	Ich bezahle nur, was auf dem Zähler steht.	ikh beht-**sah**-leh noor vahs owf daym **tsay**-ler shtayt
My change, please.	Mein Wechselgeld, bitte.	mīn **vek**-sel-gelt **bit**-teh
Keep the change.	Stimmt so.	**shtimt** zoh

Ride in style in a German taxi—usually a BMW or Mercedes. If you're having a tough time hailing a taxi, ask for the nearest taxi stand. The German word: *Taxistand*. Tipping isn't expected, but it's polite to round up. So if the fare is 19 marks, round up to 20.

Rental wheels:

I'd like to rent a...	Ich möchte ein... mieten.	ikh **murkh**-teh īn... **mee**-ten
...car.	...Auto	**ow**-toh
...station wagon.	...Kombi	**kohm**-bee
...van.	...Kleinbus	**klīn**-boos
...motorcycle.	...Motorrad	**moh**-tor-raht
...motor scooter.	...Moped	**moh**-ped
...bicycle.	...Fahrrad	**far**-raht

...tank.	...Panzer	pahn-tser
How much per...?	Wieviel pro...?	vee-feel proh
...hour	...Stunde	shtoon-deh
...day	...Tag	tahg
...week	...Woche	vokh-eh
Unlimited mileage?	Unbegrenzte Kilometer?	oon-beh-grents-teh kee-loh-may-ter
I brake for bakeries.	Ich bremse für Bäckereien.	ikh brem-zeh fewr bek-eh-rī-en
Is there a...?	Gibt es eine...?	gipt es ī-neh
...helmet	...Helm	helm
...discount	...Ermäßigung	ehr-may-see-goong
...deposit	...Kaution	kowt-see-ohn
...insurance	...Versicherung	fehr-zikh-eh-roong
When do I bring it back?	Wann bringe ich es zurück?	vahn bring-geh ikh es tsoo-rewk

Driving:

gas station	Tankstelle	tahnk-shtel-leh
The nearest gas station?	Die nächste Tankstelle?	dee nekh-steh tahnk-shtel-leh
Self-service?	Selbstbedienung?	zehlpst-beh-dee-noong
Fill the tank.	Volltanken.	fol-tahnk-en
I need...	Ich brauche...	ikh browkh-eh
...gas.	...Benzin.	ben-tseen
...unleaded.	...Bleifrei.	blī-frī
...regular.	...Normal.	nor-mahl
...super.	...Super.	zoo-per
...diesel.	...Diesel.	dee-zel

Check the...	Sehen Sie nach...	**zay**-hen zee nahkh
...oil.	...Öl.	url
...air in the tires.	...Luftdruck in Reifen.	**luft**-druk in **rī**-fen
...radiator.	...Kühler.	**kew**-ler
...battery.	...Batterie.	baht-teh-**ree**
...fuses.	...Sicherungen.	**zikh**-eh-roong-en
...sparkplugs.	...Zündkerzen.	**tsewt**-ker-tsen
...headlights.	...Scheinwerfer.	**shīn**-ver-fer
...tail lights.	...Rücklicht.	**rewk**-likht
...directional signal.	...Blinker.	**blink**-er
...car mirror.	...Rückspiegel.	**rewk**-spee-gel
...fanbelt.	...Keilriemen.	**kīl**-ree-men
...brakes.	...Bremsen.	**brem**-zen
...my pulse.	...meinem Puls.	**mī**-nem pools

Getting gas is a piece of *Strudel*. Regular is *normal* and super is *super,* and marks and liters replace dollars and gallons. If a mark is 2/3 of a dollar and there are about 4 liters in a gallon, gas costing 1.50 DM a liter = $4 a gallon.

Car trouble:

accident	**Unfall**	**oon**-fahl
breakdown	**Panne**	**pah**-neh
funny noise	**komisches Geräusch**	koh-mish-es geh-**roysh**
electrical problem	**elektrische Schwierigkeiten**	eh-**lek**-trish-eh **shvee**-rig-kī-ten
flat tire	**Reifenpanne**	**rī**-fen-pah-neh
dead battery	**leere Batterie**	**lehr**-eh baht-teh-**ree**

My car won't start.	**Mein Auto springt nicht an.**	mīn **ow**-toh shpringt nikht ahn
This doesn't work.	**Das geht nicht.**	dahs gayt nikht
It's overheating.	**Es überhitzt.**	es **ew**-behr-hitst
My car is broken.	**Mein Auto ist kaputt.**	mīn **ow**-toh ist kah-**put**
It's a lemon (useless box).	**Es ist eine Schrottkiste.**	es ist ī-neh **shroht**-kis-teh
I need a...	**Ich brauche einen...**	ikh **browkh**-eh ī-nen
...tow truck.	**...Abschleppwagen.**	**ahp**-shlep-vah-gen
...mechanic.	**...Mechaniker.**	mekh-**ahn**-i-ker
...stiff drink.	**...Schnaps.**	shnahps

For help with repair, look up "Repair" under Shopping.

Parking:

parking garage	**Garage**	gah-**rah**-zheh
Where can I park?	**Wo kann ich parken?**	voh kahn ikh **par**-ken
Is parking nearby?	**Gibt es Parkplätze in der Nähe?**	gipt es **park**-plet-seh in dehr **nay**-heh
Can I park here?	**Darf ich hier parken?**	darf ikh heer **par**-ken
How long can I park here?	**Wie lange darf ich hier parken?**	vee **lahng**-eh darf ikh heer **par**-ken
Must I pay to park here?	**Kostet Parken hier etwas?**	**kos**-tet **par**-ken heer **et**-vahs
Is this a safe place to park?	**Ist dies ein sicherer Parkplatz?**	ist deez īn **zikh**-her-er **park**-plahts

Finding your way:

I'm going to... (if you're on foot)	Ich gehe nach...	ikh **gay**-heh nahkh
I'm going to... (if you're using wheels)	Ich fahre nach...	ikh **fah**-reh nahkh
How do I get to...?	Wie komme ich nach...?	vee **kom**-meh ikh nahkh
Do you have a...?	Haben Sie eine...?	**hah**-ben zee **ī**-neh
...city map	...Stadtplan	**shtaht**-plahn
...road map	...Straßenkarte	**shtrah**-sen-kar-teh
How many minutes / hours...?	Wieviele Minuten / Stunden...?	vee-**fee**-leh mee-**noo**-ten / **shtoon**-den
...by foot	...zu Fuß	tsoo foos
...by bicycle	...mit dem Rad	mit daym raht
...by car	...mit dem Auto	mit daym **ow**-toh
How many kilometers to...?	Wieviele Kilometer sind es nach...?	vee-**fee**-leh kee-loh-**may**-ter zint es nahkh
What's the... route to Berlin?	Was ist der... Weg nach Berlin?	vahs ist dehr... vayg nahkh behr-**lin**
...best	...beste	**bes**-teh
...fastest	...schnellste	**shnel**-steh
...most interesting	...interessanteste	in-tehr-es-**sahn**-tes-teh
Point it out?	Zeigen Sie es mir?	**tsī**-gen zee es meer
I'm lost.	Ich habe mich verlaufen.	ikh **hah**-beh mikh fehr-**lowf**-en
Where am I?	Wo bin ich?	voh bin ikh
Who am I?	Wie heiße ich?	vee **hī**-seh ikh
Where is...?	Wo ist...?	voh ist
The nearest...?	Der nächste...?	dehr **nekh**-steh

| Where is this address? | **Wo ist diese Adresse?** | voh ist **dee**-zeh ah-**dres**-seh |

Key route-finding words:

city map	**Stadtplan**	**shtaht**-plahn
road map	**Straßenkarte**	**shtrah**-sen-kar-teh
downtown	**Zentrum, Stadzentrum**	**tsen**-troom, **shtaht**-tsen-troom
straight ahead	**geradeaus**	geh-**rah**-deh-**ows**
left / right	**links / rechts**	links / rekhts
first / next	**erste / nächste**	**ehr**-steh / **nekh**-steh
intersection	**Kreuzung**	**kroy**-tsoong
stoplight	**Ampel**	**ahm**-pel
roundabout	**Kreisel**	**krī**-zel
(main) square	**(Markt)platz**	**(markt)**-plahts
street	**Straße**	**shtrah**-seh
bridge	**Brücke**	**brew**-keh
tunnel	**Tunnel**	**too**-nel
highway	**Landstraße**	**lahnd**-shtrah-seh
freeway	**Autobahn**	**ow**-toh-bahn
north / south	**Nord / Süd**	nord / zewd
east / west	**Ost / West**	ost / vest

Reading German road signs:

Alle Richtungen	out of town (all destinations)
Ausfahrt	exit
Autobahn Kreuz	freeway interchange
Baustelle	construction
Dreieck	"3-corner" or fork
Einbahnstrasse	one-way street
Einfahrt	entrance

Fussgänger	pedestrians
Gebühr	toll
Langsam	slow down
Nächste Ausfart	next exit
Parken verboten	no parking
Stadtmitte	to the center of town
Stopp	stop
Strassen-arbeiten	road workers ahead
Umleitung	detour
Vorfahrt beachten	yield
Zentrum	to the center of town

Here are the standard symbols you'll see:

DUH   NO ENTRY FOR CARS   ALL VEHICLES PROHIBITED   NO ENTRY   SPEED LIMIT (IN KM)   YIELD   NO PASSING   DANGER   PARKING

The shortest distance between any two points in Germany is the *Autobahn*. The right to no speed limit is as close to the average German driver's heart as the right to bear arms is to many American hearts. To survive, never cruise in the passing lane. While all roads seem to lead to the little town of *Ausfahrt*, that is the German word for exit. The *Autobahn* information magazine, available at any *Autobahn Tankstelle* (gas station), lists all road signs, interchanges, and the hours and facilities available at various rest stops. Missing a turnoff can cost you lots of time and miles—be alert for *Autobahn Kreuz* (interchange) signs.

As in any country, the flashing lights of a patrol car are a sure sign that someone's in trouble. If it's you, try this handy phrase: *"Entschuldigung, ich bin Tourist"* (Sorry, I'm a tourist). Or, for the adventurous: *"Wenn es Ihnen nicht gefällt, wie ich Auto fahre, gehen Sie doch vom Gehweg runter."* (If you don't like how I drive, stay off the sidewalk.)

The German word for journey or trip is *Fahrt*. Many tourists enjoy collecting Fahrts. In Germany you'll see signs for *Einfahrt* (entrance), *Rundfahrt* (round trip), *Rückfahrt* (return trip), *Himmelfahrt* (ascend to heaven day, August 15th), *Panoramafahrt* (scenic journey), *Zugfahrt* (train trip), *Ausfahrt* (trip out), and throughout your trip, people will smile and wish you a *"Gute Fahrt."*

Other signs you may bump into:

belegt	no vacancy
besetzt	occupied
Bissiger Hund	mean dog
Damen	women
drücken / ziehen	push / pull
Einfahrt freihalten	keep entrance clear
Eintritt frei	free admission
Gefahr	danger
geöffnet von... bis...	open from... to...
geöffnet	open
geschlossen	closed
Herren	men
kein Eingang, keine Einfahrt	no entry
kein Trinkwasser	undrinkable water
keine Werbung	no soliciting
lebensgefährlich	extremely dangerous
nicht rauchen	no smoking

Notausgang	emergency exit
Ruhetag	closed (quiet day)
Stammtisch	reserved table for regulars
Toiletten	toilet
Verboten	forbidden
Vorsicht	caution
WC	toilet
wegen Umbau geschlossen	closed for restoration
wegen Ferien geschlossen	closed for vacation
ziehen / drücken	pull / push
Zimmer frei	rooms available
zu verkaufen	for sale
zu vermieten	for rent or for hire
Zugang verboten	keep out

Sleeping

Places to stay:

hotel	**Hotel**	hoh-**tel**
small hotel	**Pension**	pen-see-**ohn**
room in a home or bed & breakfast	**Gästezimmer, Fremdenzimmer**	**ges**-teh-tsim-mer, **frem**-den-tsim-mer
youth hostel	**Jugendherberge**	**yoo**-gend-hehr-behr-geh
vacancy	**Zimmer frei**	**tsim**-mer frī
no vacancy	**belegt**	beh-**legt**

The word *garni* in a hotel name means "without restaurant."

Reserving a room:

If you reserve a room by phone, a good time to call is the morning of the day you plan to arrive. To reserve by fax, use the nifty form in the appendix.

Hello.	**Guten Tag.**	**goo**-ten tahg
My name is...	**Ich heiße...**	ikh **hī**-seh
Do you speak English?	**Sprechen Sie Englisch?**	**shprekh**-en zee **eng**-lish
Do you have a room...?	**Haben Sie ein Zimmer...?**	**hah**-ben zee īn **tsim**-mer
...for one person	**...für eine Person**	fewr ī-neh pehr-**zohn**
...for two people	**...für zwei Personen**	fewr tsvī pehr-**zoh**-nen
...for tonight	**...für heute abend**	fewr **hoy**-teh ah-bent
...for two nights	**...für zwei Nächte**	fewr tsvī **naykh**-teh
...for Friday	**...für Freitag**	fewr frī-tahg

...for June 21	...für einund-zwanzigsten Juni	fewr īn-oont-tsvahn-tsig-ten **yoo**-nee
Yes or no?	**Ja oder nein?**	yah **oh**-der nīn
I'd like...	**Ich möchte...**	ikh **murkh**-teh
...a private bathroom.	**...eigenes Bad.**	ī-geh-nes baht
...your cheapest room.	**...ihr billigstes Zimmer.**	eer **bil**-lig-stes **tsim**-mer
...___ bed(s) for ___ people in ___ room(s).	**...___ Bett(en) für ___ Personen in ___ Zimmer(n).**	___ bet-(ten) fewr ___ pehr-**zoh**-nen in ___ **tsim**-mer(n)
How much is it?	**Wieviel kostet das?**	vee-**feel kos**-tet dahs
Anything cheaper?	**Etwas billigeres?**	et-vahs **bil**-lig-er-es
I'll take it.	**Ich nehme es.**	ikh **nay**-meh es
I'll stay for...	**Ich bleibe für...**	ikh **blī**-beh fewr
We'll stay for...	**Wir bleiben für...**	veer **blī**-ben fewr
...one night.	**...eine nacht.**	ī-neh nahkht
...___ nights.	**...___ nächte.**	___ **naykh**-teh
I'll come...	**Ich komme...**	ikh **kom**-meh
We'll come...	**Wir kommen...**	veer **kom**-men
...in one hour.	**...in einer Stunde.**	in ī-ner **shtoon**-deh
...before 16:00.	**...vor sechzehn Uhr.**	for **zekh**-tsayn oor
...Friday before 6 p.m.	**...Freitag vor sechs Uhr abends.**	**frī**-tahg for zex oor ah-**bents**
Thank you.	**Danke.**	**dahng**-keh

Getting specific:

I'd like a room...	**Ich möchte ein Zimmer...**	ikh **murkh**-teh īn **tsim**-mer
...with / without / and	**...mit / ohne / und**	mit / **oh**-neh / oont

...toilet	**...Toilette**	toh-**leh**-teh
...shower	**...Dusche**	**doo**-sheh
...shower down the hall	**...Dusche im Gang**	**doo**-sheh im gahng
...bathtub	**...Badewanne**	**bah**-deh-vah-neh
...double bed	**...Doppelbett**	**dop**-pel-bet
...twin beds	**...zwei Einzelbetten**	tsvī **īn**-tsel-bet-ten
...balcony	**...Balkon**	**bahl**-kohn
...view	**...Ausblick**	**ows**-blick
...with only a sink	**...nur mit Waschbecken**	noor mit **vahsh**-bek-en
...on the ground floor	**...im Erdgeschoß**	im **ehrd**-geh-shos
...television	**...Fernsehen**	fern-**zay**-hen
...telephone	**...Telefon**	tel-eh-**fohn**
Is there an elevator?	**Gibt es einen Fahrstuhl?**	gipt es **ī**-nen **far**-shtool
We arrive Monday, depart Wednesday.	**Wir kommen am Montag, und reisen am Mittwoch ab.**	veer **kom**-men ahm **mohn**-tahg oont **rī**-zen ahm **mit**-vokh ahp
I'll sleep anywhere. I'm desperate.	**Ich kann auf dem Fußboden schlafen. Ich bin am Verzweifeln.**	ikh kahn owf daym **foos**-boh-den **shlah**-fen. ikh bin ahm fehr-**tsvī**-feln
I have a sleeping bag.	**Ich habe einen Schlafsack.**	ikh **hah**-beh **ī**-nen **shlahf**-zahk
Will you please call another hotel?	**Rufen Sie bitte in einem anderen Hotel an?**	**roo**-fen zee **bit**-teh in **ī**-nem **ahn**-der-en **hoh**-tel ahn

Confirming, changing, and canceling reservations:

You can use this template for your telephone call.

I have a reservation.	Ich habe eine Reservierung.	ikh **hah**-beh **ī**-neh reh-zehr-**feer**-oong
My name is...	Ich heiße...	ikh **hī**-seh
I'd like to... my reservation.	Ich möchte meine Reservierung...	ikh **murkh**-teh **mī**-neh reh-zehr-**feer**-oong
...confirm	...bestätigen	beh-**shtay**-teh-gen
...reconfirm	...nochmals bestätigen	**nokh**-mahls beh-**shtay**-teh-gen
...cancel	...annullieren	ahn-nool-ee-**ehr**-en
...change	...ändern	**ayn**-dehrn
The reservation is / was for...	Die Reservierung ist / war für...	dee reh-zehr-**feer**-oong ist / vahr fewr
...one person / two people	...eine Person / zwei Personen	**ī**-neh pehr-**zohn** / tsvī pehr-**zoh**-nen
...today / tomorrow	...heute / morgen	**hoy**-teh / **mor**-gen
...August 13	...dreizehnten August	drī-tsayn-ten **ow**-gust
...one night / two nights	...eine Nacht / zwei Nächte	**ī**-neh nahkht / tsvī **naykh**-teh
Did you find my reservation?	Haben Sie meine Reservierung gefunden?	**hah**-ben zee **mī**-neh reh-zehr-**feer**-oong geh-**foon**-den
I'd like to arrive instead on...	Ich möchte lieber am... kommen.	ikh **murkh**-teh **lee**-ber ahm... **kom**-men
Is everything O.K.?	Ist alles in Ordnung?	ist **ahl**-les in **ord**-noong
Thank you. I'll see you then.	Vielen Dank. Bis dann.	**fee**-len dahngk bis dahn
I'm sorry I need to cancel.	Ich bedauere, aber ich muss annullieren.	ikh beh-**dow**-eh-reh **ah**-ber ikh moos ahn-nool-ee-**ehr**-en

SLEEPING

Nailing down the price:

How much is...?	**Wieviel kostet...?**	vee-**feel** kos-tet
...a room for ___ people	**...ein Zimmer für ___ Personen**	īn tsim-mer fewr ___ pehr-**zoh**-nen
...your cheapest room	**...ihr billigstes Zimmer**	eer **bil**-lig-stes **tsim**-mer
Breakfast included?	**Frühstück inklusive?**	frew-shtewk in-**kloo**-sev
Is breakfast required?	**Ist Frühstück Bedingung?**	ist **frew**-shtewk beh-**ding**-oong
How much without breakfast?	**Wieviel ohne Frühstück?**	vee-**feel** oh-neh frew-shtewk
Complete price?	**Vollpreis?**	fol-prīs
Is it cheaper if I...?	**Ist es billiger, wenn ich...?**	ist es **bil**-lig-er ven ikh
...pay cash	**...bar zahle**	bar tsah-leh
...stay ___ nights	**... ___ Nächte bleibe**	___ naykh-teh blī-beh
I'll stay ___ nights.	**Ich werde ___ Nächte bleiben.**	ikh vehr-deh ___ naykh-teh blī-ben

Choosing a room:

Can I see the room?	**Kann ich das Zimmer sehen?**	kahn ikh dahs **tsim**-mer zay-hen
Show me another room?	**Zeigen Sie mir ein anderes Zimmer?**	tsī-gen zee meer īn ahn-der-es **tsim**-mer
Do you have something...?	**Haben Sie etwas...?**	hah-ben zee et-vahs
...larger / smaller	**...größeres / kleineres**	grur-ser-es / klī-ner-es
...better / cheaper	**...besseres / billigeres**	bes-ser-es / bil-lig-er-es
...brighter	**...helleres**	hel-ler-es

...in the back	...nach hinten hinaus	nahkh **hin**-ten hin-**ows**
...quieter	...ruhigeres	**roo**-i-ger-es
I'll take it.	Ich nehme es.	ikh **nay**-meh es
My key.	Mein Schlüssel.	mīn **shlew**-sel
Sleep well.	Schlafen Sie gut.	**shlah**-fen zee goot
Good night.	Gute Nacht.	**goo**-teh nahkht

Hotel help:

I'd like...	Ich hätte gern...	ikh **het**-teh gehrn
...a / another	...ein / noch ein	īn / nokh īn
...towel.	...Handtuch.	**hahnd**-tookh
...pillow.	...Kissen.	**kis**-sen
...clean sheets.	...saubere Laken.	**zow**-ber-eh **lah**-ken
...blanket.	...Decke.	**dek**-eh
...glass.	...Glas.	glahs
...sink stopper.	...Abflußstöpsel	**ahp**-floos-shtohp-zel
...soap.	...Seife.	**zī**-feh
...toilet paper.	...Klopapier.	**kloh**-pah-peer
...crib.	...Kinderbett.	**kin**-der-bet
...small extra bed.	...kleines Extrabett.	**klī**-nes ehk-strah-bet
...different room.	...anderes Zimmer.	**ahn**-der-es **tsim**-mer
...silence.	...Ruhe.	**roo**-heh
Where can I wash / hang my laundry?	Wo kann ich meine Wäsche waschen / aufhängen?	voh kahn ikh **mī**-neh **vesh**-eh **vahsh**-en / **owf**-heng-en
I'd like to stay another night.	Ich möchte noch eine Nacht bleiben.	ikh **murkh**-teh nokh **ī**-neh nahkht **blī**-ben
Where can I park?	Wo soll ich parken?	voh zol ikh **par**-ken

SLEEPING

What time do you lock up?	**Um wieviel Uhr schließen Sie ab?**	oom vee-**feel** oor shlee-sen zee ahp
What time is breakfast?	**Um wieviel Uhr ist Frühstück?**	oom vee-**feel** oor ist frew-shtewk
Please wake me at 7:00.	**Wecken Sie mich um sieben Uhr, bitte.**	**vek**-en zee mikh oom **zee**-ben oor **bit**-teh

Hotel hassles:

Come with me.	**Kommen Sie mit.**	**kom**-men zee mit
I have a problem in my room.	**Es gibt ein Problem mit meinem Zimmer.**	es gipt īn proh-**blaym** mit **mī**-nem **tsim**-mer
It smells bad.	**Es stinkt.**	es shtinkt
bedbugs	**Wanzen**	**vahn**-tsen
mice	**Mäuse**	**moy**-zeh
prostitutes	**Freudenmädchen**	**froy**-den-mayd-khen
The bed is too soft / hard.	**Das Bett ist zu weich / hart.**	dahs bet ist tsoo vīkh / hart
I'm covered with bug bites.	**Ich bin mit Wanzenbissen übersäht.**	ikh bin mit **vahn**-tsen-**bis**-sen **ew**-ber-**zayt**
Lamp...	**Lampe...**	**lahm**-peh
Lightbulb...	**Birne...**	**bir**-neh
Electrical outlet...	**Steckdose...**	**shtek**-doh-zeh
Key...	**Schlüssel...**	**shlew**-sel
Lock...	**Schloß...**	shlos
Window...	**Fenster...**	**fen**-ster
Faucet...	**Wasserhahn...**	**vah**-ser-hahn
Sink...	**Waschbecken...**	**vahsh**-bek-en
Toilet...	**Klo...**	kloh
Shower...	**Dusche...**	**doo**-sheh

...doesn't work.	**...ist kaputt.**	ist kah-**put**
There is no hot water.	**Es gibt kein warmes Wasser.**	es gipt kîn **var**-mes **vahs**-ser
When is the water hot?	**Wann wird das Wasser warm?**	vahn virt dahs **vahs**-ser varm

Checking out:

I'll leave...	**Ich fahre... ab.**	ikh **fah**-reh... ahp
We'll leave...	**Wir fahren... ab.**	veer **fah**-ren... ahp
...today / tomorrow	**...heute / morgen**	**hoy**-teh / **mor**-gen
...very early	**...sehr früh**	zehr frew
When is check-out time?	**Wann muß ich das Zimmer verlassen?**	vahn mus ikh dahs **tsim**-mer fehr-**lah**-sen
Can I pay now?	**Kann ich jetzt zahlen?**	kahn ikh yetzt **tsah**-len
Bill, please.	**Rechnung, bitte.**	**rekh**-noong **bit**-teh
Credit card O.K.?	**Kreditkarte O.K.?**	kreh-**deet**-kar-teh "O.K."
I slept like a bear.	**Ich habe wie ein Bär geschlafen.**	ikh **hah**-beh vee în bar geh-**shlahf**-en
Everything was great.	**Alles war gut.**	**ahl**-les var goot
Will you call my next hotel for me?	**Können Sie mein nächstes Hotel anrufen?**	**kurn**-nen zee mîn **nekh**-stes hoh-**tel** **ahn**-roo-fen
Can I...?	**Kann ich...?**	kahn ikh
Can we...?	**Können wir...?**	**kurn**-nen veer
...leave luggage here until ___	**...das Gepäck hierlassen bis ___**	dahs geh-**pek** **heer**-lah-sen bis

Camping:

tent	**Zelt**	tselt
camping	**Camping**	**kahm**-ping
Where is a campground?	**Wo ist ein Campingplatz?**	voh ist īn **kahm**-ping-plahts
Can I...?	**Kann ich...?**	kahn ikh
Can we...?	**Können wir...?**	**kurn**-nen veer
...camp here for one night	**...hier eine Nacht zelten**	heer ī-neh nahkht **tsehl**-ten
Are showers included?	**Duschen eingeschlossen?**	**doo**-shen īn-geh-shlos-sen

Laundry:

self-service laundry	**Waschsalon**	**vahsh**-zah-lohn
wash / dry	**wasch / trocknen**	vahsh / **trok**-nen
washer / dryer	**Waschmaschine / Trockner**	vahsh-mah-**shee**-neh / **trok**-ner
detergent	**Waschmittel**	**vahsh**-mit-tel
token	**Zahlmarke, Jeton**	**tsahl**-mar-keh, **yeh**-tohn
whites / colors	**Helles / Buntwäsche**	**hel**-les / **boont**-vah-sheh
delicates	**Feinwäsche**	**fīn**-vah-sheh
handwash	**von Hand waschen**	fon hahnt **vah**-shen
How does this work?	**Wie schaft das?**	vee shahft dahs
Where is the soap?	**Wo ist die Seife?**	voh ist dee **zī**-feh
I need change.	**Ich brauche Kleingeld.**	ikh **browkh**-eh **klīn**-gelt
full-service laundry	**Waschsale mit Bedienung**	**vahsh**-zah-leh mit beh-**dee**-noong
Same-day service?	**Noch am selben Tag?**	nokh ahm **zel**-ben tahg

By when do I need to drop off my clothes?	**Bis wann kann ich meine Wäsche vorbeibringen?**	bis vahn kahn ikh mī-neh **vah**-sheh for-bī-**bring**-en
When will my clothes be ready?	**Wann wird meine Wäsche fertig sein?**	vahn virt mī-neh **vah**-sheh **fehr**-tig zīn
Dried?	**Getrocknet?**	geh-**trok**-net
Folded? ·	**Gefaltet?**	geh-**fahl**-tet

Eating

Finding a restaurant:

Where's a good... restaurant nearby?	Wo ist hier ein gutes... Restaurant?	voh ist heer īn goo-tes... res-tow-rahnt
...cheap	...billiges	bil-lig-es
...local-style	...einheimisches	īn-hī-mish-es
...untouristy	...nicht für Touristen gedachtes	nikht fewr too-ris-ten geh-dahkh-tes
...Italian	...italienisches	i-tahl-yehn-ish-es
...Turkish	...türkisches	tewrk-ish-es
...Chinese	...chinesisches	khee-nayz-ish-es
...fast food	...Schnellimbiß	shnel-im-bis
...self-service buffet	...Selbstbedienungs- buffett	zelpst-beh-dee-noongs- boo-fay
with a salad bar	mit Salatbar	mit zah-laht-bar
with terrace	mit Terrasse	mit tehr-rahs-seh
with candles	bei Kerzenlicht	bī ker-tzen-likht
romantic	romantisch	roh-mahn-tish
moderately-priced	günstig	gewn-shtig
a splurge	zum Verwöhnen	tsoom fehr-vur-nen

Getting a table and menu:

Waiter.	Kellner.	kel-ner
Waitress.	Kelinerin.	kel-ner-in
I'd like...	Ich hätte gern...	ikh het-teh gehrn
...a table for one / two.	...einen Tisch für ein / zwei.	ī-nen tish fewr īn / tsvī
...non-smoking.	...Nichtraucher.	nikht-rowkh-er
...just a drink.	...nur etwas zu trinken.	noor et-vahs tsoo trink-en

...a snack.	...eine Kleinigkeit.	ī-neh klī-nig-kīt
...just a salad.	...nur einen Salat.	noor ī-nen zah-**laht**
Can I...?	Kann ich...?	kahn ik
...see the menu	...die Karte sehen	dee **kar**-teh **zay**-hen
...order	...bestellen	beh-**shtel**-len
...pay	...zahlen	**tsahl**-en
...throw up	...mich übergeben	mik **ew**-ber-gay-ben
What do you recommend?	Was schlagen Sie vor?	vahs **shlah**-gen zee for
What's your favorite food?	Was ist ihr Lieblingsessen?	vahs ist eer **leeb**-lings-es-sen
Is it...?	Ist es...?	ist es
...good	...gut	goot
...expensive	...teuer	**toy**-er
...light	...leicht	līkht
...filling	...sättigend	**set**-tee-gend
What's cheap and filling?	Was ist billig und sättigend?	vahs ist **bil**-lig oont **set**-tee-gend
What is fast?	Was geht schnell?	vahs gayt shnel
What is local?	Was ist typisch?	vahs ist **tew**-pish
What is that?	Was ist das?	vahs ist dahs
Do you have...?	Haben Sie...?	**hah**-ben zee
...an English menu	...eine Speisekarte in englisch	ī-neh **shpī**-zeh-kar-teh in **eng**-lish
...a children's portion	...einen Kinderteller	ī-nen **kin**-der-tel-ler

In many bars and restaurants you'll see tables with little signs that say *Stammtisch* ("this table reserved for our regulars"). Don't sit there unless you're invited by a local.

The menu:

menu	**Karte, Speisekarte**	**kar**-teh, **shpī-**zeh-**kar**-teh
menu of the day	**Tageskarte**	**tah**-ges-kar-teh
tourist menu	**Touristenmenü**	too-**ris**-ten-meh-**new**
specialty of the house	**Spezialität des Hauses**	shpayt-see-ahl-ee-**tayt** des how-zes
drink menu	**Getränkekarte**	geh-**trenk**-eh-**kar**-teh
breakfast	**Frühstück**	frew-shtewk
lunch	**Mittagessen**	**mit**-tahg-es-sen
dinner	**Abendessen**	**ah**-bent-es-sen
appetizers	**Vorspeise**	for-shpī-zeh
cold plates	**Kalte Gericht**	kahlt geh-**rikht**
sandwiches	**Brotzeiten**	broht-tsī-ten
bread	**Brot**	broht
salad	**Salat**	zah-**laht**
soup	**Suppe**	**zup**-peh
first course	**erster Gang**	**ehr**-ster gahng
main course	**Hauptgerichte**	howpt-geh-**rikh**-teh
meat	**Fleisch**	flīsh
poultry	**Geflügel**	geh-**flew**-gel
fish	**Fisch**	fish
seafood	**Meeresfrüchte**	**meh**-res-frewkh-teh
side dishes	**Beilagen**	**bī**-lah-gen
vegetables	**Gemüse**	geh-**mew**-zeh
children's plate	**Kinderteller**	kin-der-tel-ler
cheese	**Käse**	**kay**-zeh
dessert	**Nachspeise**	nahkh-shpī-zeh
beverages	**Getränke**	geh-**trenk**-eh

beer	**Bier**	beer
wine	**Wein**	vīn
cover charge	**Eintritt**	**īn**-trit
service included	**mit Bedienung**	mit beh-**dee**-noong
service not included	**ohne Bedienung**	**oh**-neh beh-**dee**-noong
hot / cold	**warm / kalt**	varm / kahlt
with / without	**mit / ohne**	mit / **oh**-neh
and / or	**und / oder**	oont / **oh**-der

Dietary restrictions:

I'm allergic to...	**Ich bin allergisch gegen...**	ikh bin ah-**lehr**-gish **gay**-gen
I cannot eat...	**Ich darf kein... essen.**	ikh darf kīn... **es**-sen
...dairy products.	**...Milchprodukte**	milkh-proh-**dook**-teh
...meat.	**...Fleisch**	flīsh
...pork.	**...Schweinefleisch**	**shvī**-neh-flīsh
...salt / sugar.	**...Salz / Zucker**	zahlts / **tsoo**-ker
I'm a diabetic.	**Ich bin Diabetiker.**	ikh bin dee-ah-**bet**-i-ker
No fat.	**Ohne Fett.**	**oh**-neh fet
Minimal fat.	**Mit wenig Fett.**	mit **vay**-nig fet
Low cholesterol?	**Niedriger Cholesterin?**	**nee**-dri-ger koh-**les**-ter-in
No caffeine.	**Koffeinfrei.**	koh-fay-**in**-frī
No alcohol.	**Kein alkohol.**	kīn **ahl**-koh-hohl
I'm a...	**Ich bin...**	ikh bin
...vegetarian.	**...Vegetarier.**	veh-geh-**tar**-ee-er
...strict vegetarian.	**...strenger Vegetarier.**	**shtreng**-er veh-geh-**tar**-ee-er

| ...carnivore. | ...Fleischfresser. | flish-fres-ser |
| ...big eater. | ...grosser Esser. | groh-ser es-ser |

Tableware and condiments:

plate	Teller	tel-ler
extra plate	Extrateller	ek-strah-tel-ler
napkin	Serviette	zehr-vee-et-teh
silverware	Tafelsilber	tah-fel-sil-ber
knife	Messer	mes-ser
fork	Gabel	gah-bel
spoon	Löffel	lurf-fel
cup	Tasse	tah-seh
glass	Glas	glahs
carafe	Karaffe	kah-rah-fah
water	Wasser	vah-ser
bread	Brot	broht
large pretzels	Breze	breh-tseh
butter	Butter	but-ter
margarine	Margarine	mar-gah-ree-neh
salt / pepper	Salz / Pfeffer	zahlts / fef-fer
sugar	Zucker	tsoo-ker
artificial sweetener	Süßstoff	sews-shtohf
honey	Honig	hoh-nig
mustard...	Senf...	zenf
...mild / sharp / sweet	...mild / scharf /süß	milled / sharf / zews
mayonnaise	Mayonnaise	mah-yoh-nay-zeh
ketchup	Ketchup	"ketchup"

EATING

German restaurants close one day a week. It's called *Ruhetag* (quiet day). Before tracking down a recommended restaurant, call to make sure it's open.

Restaurant requests and regrets:

A little.	Ein bißchen.	īn **bis**-yen
More. / Another.	Mehr. / Noch ein.	mehr / nokh īn
The same.	Das gleiche.	dahs **glīkh**-eh
I did not order this.	Dies habe ich nicht bestellt.	deez **hah**-beh ikh nikht beh-**shtelt**
Is it included with the meal?	Ist das im Essen inbegriffen?	ist dahs im **es**-sen **in**-beh-grif-en
I'm in a hurry.	Ich habe wenig Zeit.	ikh **hah**-beh **vay**-nig tsīt
I must leave at ___.	Ich muß um ___ gehen.	ikh mus oom ___ **gay**-hen
When will the food be ready?	Wann ist das Essen fertig?	vahn ist dahs **es**-sen **fehr**-tig
I've changed my mind.	Ich möchte das doch nicht.	ikh **murkh**-teh dahs dokh nikht
Can I get it "to go"?	Zum Mitnehmen?	tsoom **mit**-nay-men
This is...	Dies ist...	deez ist
...dirty.	...schmutzig.	**shmut**-tsig
...too greasy.	...zu fettig.	tsoo **fet**-tig
...too salty.	...zu salzig.	tsoo **zahl**-tsig
...undercooked.	...zu wenig gekocht.	tsoo **vay**-nig geh-**kokht**
...overcooked.	...zu lang gekocht.	tsoo lahng geh-**kokht**
...inedible.	...nicht eßbar.	nikht **es**-bar
...cold.	...kalt.	kahlt
Please heat this up?	Bitte aufwärmen?	**bit**-teh **owf**-vehr-men
Enjoy your meal!	Guten Appetit!	**goo**-ten ah-peh-**teet**
Enough.	Genug.	geh-**noog**
Finished.	Fertig.	**fehr**-tig

Do any of your customers return?	Kommen ihre Kunden je zurück?	kom-men eer-eh koon-den yay tsoo-rewk
Yuck!	Igitt!	ee-git
Delicious!	Lecker!	lek-er
It tastes very good!	Schmeckt sehr gut!	shmekht zehr goot
Excellent!	Ausgezeichnet!	ows-get-sikh-net

Paying for your meal:

Waiter / Waitress.	Kellner / Kellnerin.	kel-ner / kel-ner-in
Bill, please.	Rechnung, bitte.	rekh-noong bit-teh
Separate checks.	Getrennte Rechnung.	geh-tren-teh rekh-noong
Together.	Zusammen.	tsoo-zah-men
Credit card O.K.?	Kreditkarte O.K.?	kreh-deet-kar-teh "O.K."
Is there a cover charge?	Kostet es Eintritt?	kos-tet es in-trit
This is not correct.	Dies stimmt nicht.	deez shtimt nikht
Please explain.	Erklären Sie, bitte.	ehr-klehr-en zee bit-teh
What if I wash the dishes?	Und wenn ich die Teller abwasche?	oont ven ikh dee tel-ler ahp-vah-sheh
Keep the change.	Stimmt so.	shtimt zoh
This is for you.	Dies ist für Sie.	deez ist fewr zee

When you're ready for the bill, ask for the *"Rechnung"* (reckoning). The service charge is always included. Tipping is not expected, though it's polite to round up to the next silver coin. It's also good style to say the total amount you want to pay (including tip) when you give the waiter your money.

Breakfast:

breakfast	**Frühstück**	frew-shtewk
bread	**Brot**	broht
roll (Germany, Austria)	**Brötchen, Semmel**	**brurt**-khen, **zem**-mel
toast	**Toast**	tohst
butter	**Butter**	**but**-ter
jelly	**Marmelade**	mar-meh-**lah**-deh
pastry	**Kuchen, Gebäck**	**kookh**-en, geh-**bek**
croissant	**Croissant**	kwah-**sahnt**
omelet	**Omelett**	**om**-let
eggs	**Eier**	**ī**-er
fried eggs	**Spiegeleier**	**shpee**-gel-**ī**-er
scrambled eggs	**Rühreier**	**rew**-rī-er
soft boiled / hard boiled	**weichgekocht / hartgekocht**	**vīkh**-geh-kokht / **hart**-geh-kokht
ham	**Schinken**	**shink**-en
bacon	**Speck**	shpek
cheese	**Käse**	**kay**-zeh
yogurt	**Joghurt**	**yoh**-gurt
cereal	**Cornflakes**	"cornflakes"
granola cereal	**Müsli**	**mews**-lee
milk	**Milch**	milkh
hot chocolate	**Heißer Schokolade**	**hī**-ser shoh-koh-**lah**-deh
fruit juice	**Fruchtsaft**	**frookht**-zahft
orange juice (fresh)	**Orangensaft (frischgepreßt)**	oh-**rahn**-jen-zahft (frish-geh-**prest**)
coffee / tea (see Drinking)	**Kaffee / Tee**	kah-**fay** / tee

Is breakfast included?	Ist Frühstück eingeschlossen?	ist **frew**-shtewk **in**-geh-shlos-sen

Germans have an endearing and fun-to-mimic habit of greeting others in the breakfast room with a slow, miserable *"Morgen"* (Morning). If breakfast is optional, take a walk to the *Bäckerei-Konditorei* (bakery). Germany is famous for this special cultural attraction—more varieties of bread, pastries, and cakes than you ever imagined, baked fresh every morning and throughout the day. Sometimes a café is part of a *Konditorei*. For a hearty cereal, try *Bircher Müsli*, a healthy mix of oats and nuts.

Snacks and easy lunches:

toast with ham and cheese	Toast mit Schinken und Käse	tohst mit **shink**-en oont **kay**-zeh
bread with cheese	Käsebrot	**kay**-zeh-broht
sausage with...	Wurst mit...	vurst mit
...sauerkraut	...Kraut	krowt
...bread and mustard	...Brot und Senf	broht oont zenf
vegetable platter	Gemüseplatte	geh-**mew**-zeh-plah-teh

Sandwiches:

I'd like a sandwich.	Ich möchte gern ein Sandwich.	ikh **murkh**-teh gehrn in **zahnd**-vich
cheese	Käse	**kay**-zeh
tuna	Thunfisch	**toon**-fish
chicken	Hähnchen	**hayn**-khen
turkey	Truthahn	**troot**-hahn

EATING

ham	Schinken	shink-en
salami	Salami	sah-lah-mee
egg salad	Eiersalat	ī-er-zah-laht
peanut butter and jelly	Erndnussbutter und Marmelade	ernt-noos-but-ter oont mar-mah-lahd
lettuce	Kopfsalat	kohpf-zah-laht
tomatoes	Tomaten	toh-mah-ten
onions	Zwiebeln	tsvee-beln
mustard	Senf	zenf
mayonnaise	Mayonnaise	mah-yoh-nay-zeh

Soups and salads:

soup	Suppe	zup-peh
soup of the day	Suppe des Tages	zup-peh des tahg-es
chicken broth...	Hühnerbrühe...	hew-ner-brew-heh
beef broth...	Rinderbrühe...	rin-der-brew-heh
...with noodles	...mit Nudeln	mit noo-deln
...with rice	...mit Reis	mit rīs
vegetable soup	Gemüsesuppe	geh-mew-zeh-zup-peh
goulash soup	Gulaschsuppe	goo-lahsh-zup-peh
liver dumpling soup	Leberknödelsuppe	lay-ber-kuh-nur-del-zup-peh
green salad	grüner Salat	grew-ner zah-laht
mixed salad	gemischter Salat	geh-mish-ter zah-laht
potato salad	Kartoffelsalat	kar-tof-fel-zah-laht
Greek salad	Griechischer Salat	greekh-ish-er zah-laht
chef's salad...	gemischter Salat des Hauses...	geh-mish-ter zah-laht des how-zes
...with ham and cheese	...mit Schinken und Käse	mit shink-en oont kay-zeh

...with egg	...mit Ei	mit ī
lettuce	Salat	zah-laht
tomatoes	Tomaten	toh-mah-ten
cucumber	Gurken	gur-ken
oil / vinegar	Öl / Essig	url / es-sig
salad dressing	Salatsoße	zah-laht-zoh-seh
dressing on the side	Salatsoße extra	zah-laht-zoh-seh ehk-strah
What is in this salad?	Was ist in diesem Salat?	vahs ist in dee-zem zah-laht

The *Salatbar* (salad bar) is a global phenomenon. Budget travelers eat cheap and healthy by grabbing a plate and stacking it high. You'll normally be charged by the size of the plate for one load. Choose a *Teller* (plate) that is *kleiner* (small), *mittlerer* (medium), or *großer* (large). A small plate with a salad "pagoda" can make a fine and filling lunch.

EATING

Fish:

fish	Fisch	fish
tuna	Thunfisch	tun-fish
herring	Hering	hehr-ing
clams	Muscheln	moo-sheln
cod	Dorsch	dorsh
trout	Forelle	foh-rel-leh
pike	Hecht	hekht
salmon	Lachs	lahkhs
seafood	Meeresfrüchte	meh-res-frewkh-teh
assorted seafood	gemischte Meeresfrüchte	geh-mish-teh meh-res-frewkh-teh

| Where did this live? | Wo hat dieses Tier gelebt? | voh haht **dee**-zes teer geh-**laypt** |
| Just the head, please. | **Nur den Kopf, bitte.** | noor dayn kopf **bit**-teh |

Poultry and meat:

poultry	**Geflügel**	geh-**flew**-gel
chicken	**Hähnchen**	**haynkh**-en
roast chicken	**Brathähnchen**	**braht**-hayn-khen
turkey	**Pute**	**poo**-teh
duck	**Ente**	**en**-teh
meat	**Fleisch**	flīsh
mixed grill	**Grillteller**	**gril**-tel-ler
beef	**Rindfleisch**	rint-**flīsh**
roast beef	**Rinderbraten**	**rin**-der-brah-ten
beef steak	**Beefsteak**	**beef**-shtayk
veal	**Kalbfleisch**	**kahlp**-flīsh
cutlet	**Kotelett**	**kot**-let
pork	**Schweinefleisch**	shvī-neh-flīsh
ham	**Schinken**	**shink**-en
sausage	**Wurst**	vurst
bacon	**Speck**	shpek
lamb	**Lamm**	lahm
bunny	**Kaninchen**	kah-**neen**-khen
organs	**Innereien**	in-neh-rī-en
brains	**Hirn**	hern
liver	**Leber**	**lay**-ber
tripe	**Kutteln**	**kut**-teln
How long has this been dead?	**Wie lange ist dieses Tier schon tot?**	vee **lahng**-eh ist **dee**-zes teer shohn toht

How it's prepared:

hot / cold	**heiß / kalt**	hīs / kahlt
raw / cooked	**roh / gekocht**	roh / geh-**kokht**
assorted	**gemischte**	geh-**mish**-teh
baked	**gebacken**	geh-**bah**-ken
boiled	**gekocht**	geh-**kokht**
deep-fried	**frittiert**	frit-ti-ert
fillet	**Filet**	fi-**lay**
fresh	**frisch**	frish
fried	**gebraten**	geh-**brah**-ten
grilled	**gegrillt**	geh-**grilt**
homemade	**hausgemachte**	hows-geh-**mahkh**-teh
in cream sauce	**in Rahmsauce**	in **rahm**-zohs
microwave	**Mikrowelle**	**mee**-kroh-vel-leh
mild	**mild**	milled
mixed	**gemischte**	geh-**mish**-teh
poached	**pochierte**	pohkh-ee-**ehr**-teh
roast	**Braten**	**brah**-ten
roasted	**geröstet**	geh-**rurs**-tet
smoked	**geräuchert**	geh-**roykh**-ert
spicy hot	**scharf**	sharf
steamed	**gedünstet**	geh-**dewn**-stet
stuffed	**gefüllt**	geh-**fewlt**
sweet	**süß**	zews

Avoiding mis-steaks:

raw	**roh**	roh
rare	**halbgar**	**hahlp**-gar
medium	**mittel**	**mit**-tel
well-done	**durchgebraten**	**durkh**-geh-brah-ten
almost burnt	**fast verkohlt**	fahst fehr-**kohlt**

Styles of cooking:

art	style of cooking
Bauern	farmer style, with potatoes (good and hearty)
Jäger	hunter style, with mushrooms and gravy
Wiener	Viennese, breaded and fried
Französisch	French
Italienisch	Italian

Eating Italian in Germany:

Italian restaurants provide a good budget break from *wurst und kraut*. Here are the words you'll find on the menu: *Spaghetti, Pizza, Tomaten, Schinken* (ham), *Käse* (cheese), *Champignons* (mushrooms), *Paprika* (peppers), *Ei* (egg), *Pepperoni* (small hot peppers), *Zwiebeln* (onions), *Artischocken* (artichokes), *Basilikum* (basil), *Meeresfrüchte* (seafood), *Muscheln* (clams), and *Vegetaria* (vegetarian).

German specialties:

Brotzeit-Teller	plate of assorted meats and cheeses
Fleischfondue	meat cubes cooked in a pot of boiling oil and dipped in sauces
Fondue (Switz.)	bread cubes dipped in a mixture of melted cheese and white wine
Handkäse	curd cheese
Knödel	dense dumpling
Leberkäse	high quality Spam
Maultaschen	meat- or cheese-filled ravioli (grilled or in soup)
Raclette (Switz.)	melted cheese, ham, boiled potatoes, and pickle
Rösti (Switz.)	hashbrowns
Sauerbraten	braised beef, marinated in vinegar
Schlachtplatte	assorted cold meats (schlachten = slaughter, Schlacht = battle)
Schnitzel	thin slice of pork or veal, usually breaded
Schwarzwälder Schinken	smoked, cured ham
Spargel	white asparagus, considered a delicacy, celebrated in May and June when fresh (frisch), served in soup or on plate with cream sauce

EATING

The best of the wurst:

Blutwurst	made from (gulp!) blood
Bratwurst	pork sausage, 2 inches in diameter, grilled or fried
Nürnberger	spicy pork sausage, grilled or fried, smaller than a hot dog
Schweinswurst	pork sausage

Weisswurst	white boiled veal that falls apart when you cut it. Don't eat the skin!
mit Brot	with bread
mit Kraut	with sauerkraut

Side dishes:

vegetables	**Gemüse**	geh-**mew**-zeh
rice	**Reis**	rîs
spaghetti	**Spaghetti**	shpah-**geh**-tee
noodles	**Nudeln**	**noo**-deln
boiled German-style noodles	**Spätzle**	**shpets**-leh
liver / bread...	**Leber / Semmel...**	**lay**-ber / **zem**-mel
...dumplings	**...knödel**	kuh-**nur**-del
sauerkraut	**Sauerkraut**	"sauerkraut"
potatoes	**Kartoffeln**	kar-**tof**-feln
French fries	**Pommes frites**	pom frits
potato salad	**Kartoffelsalat**	kar-**tof**-fel-zah-laht
green salad	**grüner Salat**	**grew**-ner zah-**laht**
mixed salad	**gemischter Salat**	geh-**mish**-ter zah-**laht**

Veggies and beans:

vegetables	**Gemüse**	geh-**mew**-zeh
mixed vegetables	**gemischtes Gemüse**	geh-**mish**-tes geh-**mew**-zeh
artichoke	**Artischocke**	art-i-**shoh**-keh
asparagus	**Spargel**	**shpar**-gel
beans	**Bohnen**	**boh**-nen
beets	**Rote Beete**	**roh**-teh **bee**-teh

broccoli	**Brokkoli**	**brok**-koh-lee
cabbage	**Kohl**	kohl
carrots	**Karotten**	kah-**rot**-ten
cauliflower	**Blumenkohl**	**bloo**-men-kohl
corn	**Mais**	mīs
cucumber	**Gurken**	**gur**-ken
eggplant	**Auberginen**	**oh**-behr-zhee-nen
French fries	**Pommes frites**	pom frits
garlic	**Knoblauch**	kuh-**noh**-blowkh
green beans	**grüne Bohnen**	**grew**-neh **boh**-nen
lentils	**Linsen**	**lin**-zen
mushrooms	**Champignons**	**shahm**-pin-yohn
olives	**Oliven**	oh-**leev**-en
onions	**Zwiebeln**	**tsvee**-beln
peas	**Erbsen**	**ehrb**-zen
pepper...	**Paprika...**	**pah**-pree-kah
...green / red / yellow	**...grün / rot / gelb**	grewn / roht / gelp
pickles	**Essiggurken**	**es**-sig-goor-ken
potatoes	**Kartoffeln**	kar-**tof**-feln
radishes	**Radieschen**	rah-**dee**-shen
spinach	**Spinat**	**shpee**-naht
tomatoes	**Tomaten**	toh-**mah**-ten
zucchini	**Zucchini**	**tsoo**-kee-nee

EATING

If you knead bread:

bread	**Brot**	broht
dark bread	**Vollkornbrot**	**fol**-korn-broht
three-grain bread	**Dreikornbrot**	**drī**-korn-broht
rye bread	**Roggenmischbrot**	**roh**-gen-mish-broht
dark rye bread	**Schwarzbrot**	**shvartz**-broht

whole wheat bread	**Graubrot**	**grow**-broht
light bread	**Weißbrot**	**vīs**-broht
wimpy white bread	**Toast**	tohst
French bread	**Baguette**	bah-**get**
roll (Germany, Austria)	**Brötchen, Semmel**	**brurt**-khen, **zem**-mel

Say cheese:

cheese	**Käse**	**kay**-zeh
mild / sharp	**mild / scharf**	milled / sharf
cheese platter	**Käseplatte**	**kay**-zeh-**plah**-teh
gorgonzola	**Gorgonzola**	**gor**-gon-tsoh-lah
bleu cheese	**Blaukäse**	**blow**-kay-zeh
cream cheese	**Frischkäse**	**frish**-kay-zeh
Swiss cheese	**Emmentaler**	**em**-men-tah-ler
a strong cheese	**Bergkäse**	**berg**-kay-zeh
Can I taste it?	**Kann ich probieren?**	kahn ikh **proh**-beer-en

Fruits and nuts:

almond	**Mandel**	**mahn**-del
apple	**Apfel**	**ahp**-fel
apricot	**Aprikose**	ahp-ri-**koh**-zeh
banana	**Banane**	bah-**nah**-neh
berries	**Beeren**	**behr**-en
canteloupe	**Melone**	meh-**loh**-neh
cherry	**Kirsche**	**keer**-sheh
chestnut	**Kastanie**	**kahs**-tah-nee
coconut	**Kokosnuß**	**koh**-kohs-noos
date	**Dattel**	**daht**-tel

fig	**Feige**	**fi**-geh
fruit	**Obst**	ohpst
grapefruit	**Pampelmuse,** **Grapefruit**	pahm-pel-**moo**-zeh, **grahp**-froot
grapes	**Trauben**	**trow**-ben
hazelnut	**Haselnuß**	**hah**-zel-noos
lemon	**Zitrone**	tsee-**troh**-neh
orange	**Apfelsine**	ahp-fel-**zee**-neh
peach	**Pfirsich**	**feer**-zikh
peanut	**Erdnuß**	**ehrd**-noos
pear	**Birne**	**beer**-neh
pineapple	**Ananas**	**ahn**-ahn-ahs
pistachio	**Pistazien**	pis-**tahts**-ee-en
plum	**Pflaume**	**flow**-meh
prune	**Backpflaume**	**bahk**-flow-meh
raspberry	**Himbeere**	**him**-behr-eh
red currants	**Johannisbeeren**	yoh-**hahn**-nis-behr-en
strawberry	**Erdbeere**	**ehrt**-behr-eh
tangerine	**Mandarine**	mahn-dah-**ree**-neh
walnut	**Wallnuß**	**vahl**-noos
watermelon	**Wassermelone**	**vah**-ser-meh-loh-neh

Teutonic treats:

dessert	**Nachspeise**	**nahkh**-shpi-zeh
strudel	**Strudel**	**shtroo**-del
cake	**Kuchen**	**kookh**-en
sherbet	**Sorbet**	**zor**-bet
fruit cup	**Früchtebecher**	**frewkh**-teh-bekh-er

tart	**Törtchen**	**turt**-khen
pie	**Torte**	**tor**-teh
cream	**Schlag**	shlahg
whipped cream	**Schlagsahne**	**shlahg**-zah-neh
chocolate mousse	**Mousse**	moos
pudding	**Pudding**	"pudding"
pastry	**Gebäck**	geh-**bek**
cookies	**Kekse**	**kayk**-zeh
candy	**Bonbons**	**bon**-bonz
low calorie	**kalorienarm**	kah-loh-**ree**-en-arm
homemade	**hausgemacht**	**hows**-geh-mahkht
Delicious!	**Köstlich! Lecker!**	**kurst**-likh / **lek**-er
Heavenly.	**Himmlisch.**	**him**-lish
I'm in seventh heaven.	**Ich bin im siebten Himmel.**	ikh bin im **zeeb**-ten **him**-mel

Ice cream:

ice cream	**Eis**	īs
scoop	**Kugel**	**koog**-el
cone	**Waffel**	**vah**-fel
small bowl	**Becher**	**bekh**-er
chocolate	**Schokolade**	shoh-koh-**lah**-deh
vanilla	**Vanille**	vah-**nil**-leh
strawberry	**Erdbeere**	**ehrt**-behr-eh
lemon	**Zitrone**	tsee-**troh**-neh
rum-raisin	**Malaga**	**mah**-lah-gah
hazelnut	**Haselnuß**	**hah**-zel-noos
Can I taste it?	**Kann ich probieren?**	kahn ikh **proh**-beer-en

Two great dessert specialties are Vienna's famous super chocolate cake, *Sachertorte,* and the Black Forest cherry cake called *Schwarzwälder Kirschtorte.* This diet-killing chocolate cake with cherries and rum can be found all over Germany. Chocoholics can pick up a jar of Nutella at any grocery store. Anything dipped in Nutella becomes a tasty souvenir. For a little bit of Italy, try *gelato* (Italian ice cream) at a *gelateria.*

Drinking

Water and juice:

mineral water...	**Mineralwasser...**	min-eh-**rahl**-vah-ser
...with / without carbonation	**...mit / ohne Gas, Sprudel**	mit / **oh**-neh gahs, **shproo**-del
mixed with mineral water	**gespritzt**	geh-**shpritzt**
tap water	**Leitungswasser**	**lī**-toongs-vah-ser
Fanta & Coke mix	**Mezzo Mix, Spezi**	met-soh mix, **shpet**-see
fruit juice	**Fruchtsaft**	**frookht**-zahft
apple juice	**Apfelsaft**	**ahp**-fel-zahft
orange juice (fresh)	**Orangensaft (frischgepreßt)**	oh-**rahn**-jen-zahft (frish-geh-**prest**)
with / without...	**mit / ohne...**	mit / **oh**-neh
...ice / sugar	**...Eis / Zucker**	īs / **tsoo**-ker
glass / cup	**Glas / Tasse**	glahs / **tah**-seh
small / large bottle	**kleine / große Flasche**	**klī**-neh / **groh**-seh flah-sheh
Is the water safe to drink?	**Ist das Trinkwasser?**	ist dahs **trink**-vahs-ser

On a menu, you'll find drinks listed under *Getränkekarte* (drink menu). If you ask for *Wasser* in a restaurant, you'll be served mineral water. Free tap water is *Leitungswasser*. Germans normally don't drink this at the table. If you want *Leitungswasser*, be persistent.

Milk:

milk	**Milch**	milkh
whole milk	**Vollmilch**	**fol**-milkh
skim milk	**Magermilch**	**mah**-ger-milkh
fresh milk	**frische Milch**	**frish**-eh milkh
acidophilus	**acidophilus, kefir**	ah-see-**dof**-i-lus, **keh**-feer
buttermilk	**Buttermilch**	**but**-ter-milkh
chocolate milk	**Schokomilch**	**shoh**-koh-milkh
hot chocolate	**Kakao**	**kah**-kow
milkshake	**Milchshake**	**milkh**-shayk

Coffee and tea:

coffee	**Kaffee**	kah-**fay**
espresso	**Espresso**	es-**pres**-soh
cappuccino	**Cappuccino**	kah-poo-**chee**-noh
iced coffee	**Eiskaffee**	**īs**-kah-fay
instant	**Pulverkaffee, Nescafe**	pool-ver-kah-**fay,** "nescafe"
decaffeinated	**koffeinfrei, Hag**	koh-fay-**in**-frī, hahg
black	**schwarz**	shvarts
with cream / milk	**mit Sahne / Milch**	mit **zah**-neh / milkh
with sugar	**mit Zucker**	mit **tsoo**-ker
hot water	**heißes Wasser**	**hī**-ses **vah**-ser
tea / lemon	**Tee / Zitrone**	tee / tsee-**troh**-neh
tea bag	**Teebeutel**	**tee**-boy-tel
iced tea	**Eistee**	**īs**-tee
herbal tea	**Kräutertee**	**kroy**-ter-tee

EATING

fruit tea	**Früchte Tee**	**frewkh**-teh tee
little pot	**Kännchen**	**kaynkh**-en
small / big	**klein / groß**	klīn / grohs
Another cup.	**Noch eine Tasse.**	nokh ī-neh **tah**-seh

In Austria, coffee has a language of its own. Ask for a *Brauner* to get coffee with cream, a *Melange* for coffee with lots of milk, a *Mokka* for black espresso, and *Obers* for cream.

Wine:

I would like...	**Ich hätte gern...**	ikh **het**-teh gehrn
We would like...	**Wir hätten gern...**	veer **het**-ten gehrn
...an eighth liter	**...ein Achtel**	īn **ahkh**-tel
...a quarter liter	**...ein Viertel**	īn **feer**-tel
...a carafe	**...eine Karaffe**	ī-neh kah-**rah**-feh
...a half bottle	**...eine halbe Flasche**	ī-neh **hahl**-beh **flah**-sheh
...a bottle	**...eine Flasche**	ī-neh **flah**-sheh
...of red wine	**...Rotwein**	**roht**-vīn
...of white wine	**...Weißwein**	**vīs**-vīn
...the wine list	**...die Weinkarte**	dee **vīn**-kar-teh

Typically you order a glass of wine by saying *"Ein Viertel"* (a quarter liter) or *"Ein Achtel"* (eighth liter).

Wine words:

| wine | **Wein** | vīn |
| table wine | **Tafelwein** | **tah**-fel-vīn |

house wine	**Hausmarke**	**hows**-mar-keh
local	**einheimisch**	īn-hī-mish
red wine	**Rotwein**	**roht**-vīn
white wine	**Weißwein**	**vīs**-vīn
rosé	**rosé**	roh-**zay**
sparkling	**sprudelnd**	**shproo**-delnd
sweet	**süß**	zews
medium	**halbtrocken**	**hahlp**-trok-en
(very) dry	**(sehr) trocken**	(zehr) **trok**-en
wine spritzer	**Wein gespritzt**	vīn geh-**shpritzt**
cork	**Korken**	**kor**-ken

Types of German wines and alcohol:

Apfelwein	apple wine (Frankfurt)
Spätlese, Auslese, Beerenauslese, Trockenbeeren Auslese, Eiswein	sweet late harvest wines (listed from sweet to sweetest)
Kabinett	select wine
Qualitätswein	better quality wine
Qualitätswein mit Prädikat	best quality wine
Grüner Veltliner	popular Austrian wine
Heuriger (Austria)	new wine
Glühwein	hot spiced wine
Jagertea	half tea and half brandy & rum
Schnaps	high-alcohol brandy (firewater!)
Kirschschnaps	high-alcohol cherry brandy

Nearly all German wines are white. You can identify the origin of the wine by the color or shape of the bottle: brown (Rhine), green (Mosel), jug-shaped (Franconian). As you travel through wine-growing regions, you'll see *probieren* signs inviting you in for a free (or nearly free) wine tasting.

EATING

Beer:

beer	**Bier**	beer
from the tap	**vom Faß**	fom fahs
bottle	**Flasche**	**flah**-sheh
light--but not "lite" (Germany, Austria)	**helles, Märzen**	**hel**-les, **mehr**-tzen
dark	**dunkles**	**doonk**-les
local / imported	**einheimisch / importiert**	**īn**-hī-mish / im-por-tee-**ert**
small / large	**kleines / großes**	**klī**-nes / **groh**-ses
half-liter	**Halbes**	**hahl**-bes
liter (Bavarian)	**Mass**	mahs
alcohol-free	**alkoholfrei**	ahl-koh-hohl-**frī**
low calorie	**Light**	"light"
cold / colder	**kalt / kälter**	kahlt / **kel**-ter

Germany is Europe's beer capital. *Pils* is barley-based and *Weizen* is wheat-based. *Malzbier* is the non-alcoholic malt beer that children learn on. The barely alcoholic *Nährbier*, considered healthy and caloric, is for fattening up skinny kids. *Radler* (which means biker) is a refreshing mix of beer and lemonade, invented in Munich for cyclists on hot days. A *Berliner Weisse mit Schuß* is a wheat beer with a shot of fruit syrup. Drink menus list exactly how many deciliters you'll get in your glass. A "5 dl" beer is half a liter or about a pint. When you order beer, ask for *"Ein Halbes"* for a half liter or *"Ein Mass"* for a whole liter. Some beer halls serve beer only by the liter (about a quart)! Children are welcome in beer halls.

Bar talk:

What would you like?	**Was darf ich bringen?**	vahs darf ikh **bring**-en
What is the local specialty?	**Was ist die Spezialität hier?**	vahs ist dee **shpayt**-see-ahl-ee-**tayt** heer
Straight.	**Pur.**	poor
With / Without...	**Mit / Ohne...**	mit / **oh**-neh
...alcohol.	**...Alkohol.**	**ahl**-koh-hohl
...ice.	**...Eis.**	īs
One more.	**Noch eins.**	nokh īns
Cheers!	**Prost!**	prohst
To your health!	**Auf ihre Gesundheit!**	owf **eer**-eh geh-**zoond**-hīt
To you!	**Zum Wohl!**	tsoom vohl
Long life!	**Langes Leben!**	**lahng**-es **lay**-ben
I'm feeling...	**Ich bin...**	ikh bin
...a little drunk.	**...ein bißchen betrunken.**	īn **bis**-yen beh-**trunk**-en
...blitzed. (completely blue)	**...völlig blau.**	**furl**-lig blow

For drinks at reasonable prices, do what the locals do. Visit an atmospheric *Weinstube* (wine bar) or *Biergarten* (beer garden) and have a drink and chat with friends.

Picnicking

At the grocery:

Self-service?	**Selbstbedienung?**	**zelpst**-beh-dee-noong
Ripe for today?	**Jetzt reif?**	yetst rif
Does this need to be cooked?	**Muß man das kochen?**	mus mahn dahs **kokh**-en
Can I taste it?	**Kann ich probieren?**	kahn ik proh-**beer**-en
Fifty grams.	**Fünfzig Gramm.**	**fewnf**-tsig grahm
One hundred grams.	**Hundert Gramm.**	**hoon**-dert grahm
More. / Less.	**Mehr. / Weniger.**	mehr / **vay**-nig-er
A piece.	**Ein Stück.**	in shtewk
A slice.	**Eine Scheibe.**	**i**-neh **shi**-beh
Sliced.	**In Scheiben.**	in **shi**-ben
A small bag.	**Eine kleine Tüte.**	**i**-neh **klin**-eh **tew**-teh
A bag, please.	**Eine Tüte, bitte.**	**i**-neh **tew**-teh **bit**-teh
Can you make me a sandwich?	**Können Sie mir ein Sandwich machen?**	**kurn**-nen zee meer in **zahnd**-vich **mahkh**-en
To take out.	**Zum Mitnehmen.**	tsoom **mit**-nay-men
Is there a park nearby?	**Gibt es einen Park in der Nähe?**	gipt es **i**-nen park in dehr **nay**-heh
Okay to picnic here?	**Darf man hier picknicken?**	darf mahn heer **pik**-nik-en
Enjoy your meal!	**Guten Appetit!**	**goo**-ten ah-peh-**teet**

Assemble your picnic at a *Markt* (open air market) or *Supermarkt* (supermarket)—or get a fast snack at an *Obst* (fruit stand) or *Imbiss* (fast food stand).

At the grocery, you buy meat and cheese by the gram.

One hundred grams is about a quarter pound, enough for two sandwiches. To weigh and price your produce, put it on the scale, push the photo or number (keyed to the bin it came from), and then stick your sticker on the food. To get real juice, look for "100%" or "kein Zucker" on the label. "Drink" or "Trunk" is pop.

Tasty picnic words:

open air market	**Markt**	markt
grocery store	**Lebensmittelgeschäft**	lay-bens-mit-tel-geh-**sheft**
supermarket	**Supermarkt**	**zoo**-per-markt
picnic	**Picknick**	**pik**-nik
sandwich	**Sandwich**	**zahnd**-vich
bread	**Brot**	broht
roll (Germany, Austria)	**Brötchen, Semmel**	**brurt**-khen, **zem**-mel
sausage	**Wurst**	vurst
ham	**Schinken**	**shink**-en
cheese	**Käse**	**kay**-zeh
mild / sharp / sweet	**mild / scharf / süß**	milled / sharf / zews
mustard...	**Senf...**	zenf
mayonnaise...	**Mayonnaise...**	mah-yoh-**nay**-zeh
...in a tube	**...in der Tube**	in dehr **too**-beh
yogurt	**Joghurt**	**yoh**-gurt
fruit	**Obst**	ohpst
box of juice	**Karton Saft**	**kar**-ton zaft
cold drinks	**kalte Getränke**	**kahl**-teh geh-**trenk**-eh
plastic...	**Plastik...**	**plahs**-tik
...spoon / fork	**...löffel / gabel**	**lurf**-fel / **gah**-bel
paper...	**Papier...**	pah-**peer**
...plate / cup	**...teller / becher**	**tel**-ler / **bekh**-er

German-English Menu Decoder

This handy decoder won't list every word on the menu, but it'll get you *Bratwurst* (pork sausage) instead of *Blutwurst* (blood sausage).

Abendessen dinner
Achtel eighth liter
Ananas pineapple
Apfel apple
Apfelsaft apple juice
Apfelsine orange
Aprikose apricot
Artischocke artichoke
Aubergine eggplant
Backpflaume prune
Banane banana
Bauern with potatoes
Becher small bowl
Bedienung service
Beeren berries
Beilagen side dishes
Bier beer
Birne pear
Blumenkohl cauliflower
Blutwurst blood sausage
Bohnen beans
braten roast
Brathähnchen roast chicken
Bratwurst pork sausage
Bretzeln pretzels
Brokkoli broccoli
Brot bread

Brötchen roll
Brotzeit snack
Butterhörnchen croissant
Champignons mushrooms
chinesisches Chinese
Dattel date
Dorsch cod
dunkles dark
Ei egg
Eier eggs
einheimisch local
Eintritt cover charge
Eis ice cream
Eiskaffee iced coffee
Eistee iced tea
Ente duck
Erbsen peas
Erdbeere strawberry
Erdnuß peanut
erster Gang first course
Essen food
Essig vinegar
Essiggurken pickles
Feige fig
Fett fat
Fisch fish
Flasche bottle

Fleisch   meat
Forelle   trout
Französisch   French
frisch   fresh
frischgepreßt   freshly squeezed
Frittaten   sliced pancakes
frittiert   deep-fried
Früchtebecher   fruit cup
Fruchtsaft   fruit juice
Frühstück   breakfast
Gang   course
Gebäck   pastry
gebraten   fried
gedünstet   steamed
Geflügel   poultry
gefüllt   stuffed
gegrillt   grilled
gekocht   cooked
Gelee   jelly
gemischte   mixed
Gemüse   vegetables
Gemüseplatte   vegetable platter
geräuchert   smoked
geröstet   roasted
gespritzt   with mineral water
Getränke   beverages
Getränkekarte   drink menu
Glas   glass
Graubrot   whole wheat bread
Grillteller   mixed grill
groß   big
grüner   green
Gurken   cucumber
Hähnchen   chicken

halb   half
hartgekocht   hard-boiled
Haselnuß   hazelnut
Hauptspeise   main course
Haus   house
hausgemachte   homemade
heiß   hot
helles   light (beer)
Hering   herring
Himbeere   raspberry
Honig   honey
Hühnerbrühe   chicken broth
importiert   imported
inklusive   included
Innereien   organs
Italienisch   Italian
Jäger   with mushrooms and gravy
Joghurt   yogurt
Johannisbeeren   red currant
Kaffee   coffee
Kakao   cocoa
Kalbfleisch   veal
kalt   cold
Kaninchen   bunny
Kännchen   small pot of tea
Karaffe   carafe
Karotten   carrots
Karte   menu
Kartoffeln   potatoes
Käse   cheese
Käseplatte   cheese platter
Kastanie   chestnut
Kekse   cookies
Kinderteller   children's portion

MENU DECODER

Kirsche cherry
klein small
Kleinigkeit snack
Knoblauch garlic
Knödel dumpling
Kohl cabbage
Kohlensäure carbonation
Kokosnuß coconut
köstlich delicious
Kotelett cutlet
Kraut sauerkraut
Kräutertee herbal tea
Kugel scoop
Kutteln tripe
Lamm lamb
Leber liver
leicht light
Linsen lentils
Mais corn
Malaga rum-raisin flavor
Mandarine tangerine
Mandel almond
Mass liter of beer
Maultaschen ravioli
Meeresfrüchte seafood
Melone canteloupe
Miesmuscheln mussels
Mikrowelle microwave
Milch milk
mild mild
Mineralwasser mineral water
mit with
Mittagessen lunch
Muscheln clams

Müsli granola cereal
Nachspeise dessert
Nudeln noodles
Obst fruit
oder or
ohne without
Öl oil
Oliven olives
Omelett omelet
Orangensaft orange juice
Pampelmuse grapefruit
Paprika bell pepper
Pfeffer pepper
Pfirsich peach
Pflaume plum
Pistazien pistachio
pochieren poached
Pommes frites French fries
Pute turkey
Raclette potatoes and cheese
(Switz.)
Radieschen radishes
Rahmsauce cream sauce
Rinderbraten roast beef
Rinderbrühe beef broth
Rindfleisch beef
Roggenmischbrot rye bread
roh raw
Rösti hashbrowns (Switz.)
Rote Beete beets
Rotwein red wine
Rührei scrambled eggs
Salat salad
Salatsoße salad dressing

Salz salt
sättigend filling
Sauerbraten braised beef
Schalentiere shellfish
scharf spicy
Scheibe slice
Schinken ham
Schlachtplatte assorted cold meats
Schlag cream
Schlagsahne whipped cream
schnell fast
Schnellimbiss fast food
Schnitzel thinly-sliced pork or veal
Schokolade chocolate
Schwarzbrot dark rye bread
Schweinefleisch pork
sehr very
Semmel roll
Senf mustard
Sorbet sherbet
Spargel asparagus
Spätzle German-style noodles
Speck bacon
Spezialität speciality
Spiegeleier fried eggs
Spinat spinach
sprudelnd sparkling
Stück piece
Suppe soup
süß sweet
Tage day
Tageskarte menu of the day
Tasse cup

Tee tea
Teller plate
Thunfisch tuna
Tomaten tomatoes
Törtchen tart
Torte cake
Trauben grapes
trocken dry
typisch local
und and
Vanille vanilla
Vegetarier vegetarian
Viertel quarter liter
Vollkornbrot dark bread
Vorspeise appetizers
Waffel cone
Wallnuß walnut
Wasser water
Wassermelone watermelon
weichgekocht soft-boiled
Wein wine
Weinkarte wine list
Weißwein white wine
Wiener breaded and fried
Wiesswurst boiled veal sausage
Wurst sausage
Zitrone lemon
Zuccini zucchini
Zucker sugar
zum Mitnehman "to go"
Zwiebelbraten pot roast with onions
Zwiebeln onions

MENU DECODER

Sightseeing

Where is...?	Wo ist...?	voh ist
...the best view	...der beste Ausblick	dehr **bes**-teh **ows**-blick
...the main square	...der Hauptplatz	dehr **howpt**-plahts
...the old town center	...die Altstadt	dee **ahlt**-shtaht
...the museum	...das Museum	dahs moo-**zay**-um
...the castle	...die Burg	dee burg
...the palace	...das Schloß	dahs shlos
...the ruins	...die Ruine	dee roo-**ee**-neh
...the tourist information office	...das Touristen-Informationsbüro	dahs **too**-ris-ten-in-for-**maht**-see-ohns-**bew**-roh
...the toilet	...die Toilette	dee toh-**leh**-teh
...the entrance / exit	...der Eingang / Ausgang	dehr **īn**-gahng / **ows**-gahng
Nearby is there a...?	Gibt es in der Nähe ein...?	gipt es in dehr **nay**-heh īn
...fair (rides, games)	...Jahrmarkt	**yar**-markt
...festival (music)	...Festival	fes-tee-**vahl**
Do you have...?	Haben Sie...?	**hah**-ben zee
...a city map	...einen Stadtplan	**ī**-nen **shtaht**-plahn
...brochures	...Broschüren	broh-**shewr**-en
...guidebooks	...Führer	**fewr**-er
...tours	...Führungen	**few**-roong-en
...in English	...auf englisch	owf **eng**-lish
When is the next tour in English?	Wann ist die nächste Führung auf englisch?	vahn ist dee **nekh**-steh **few**-roong owf **eng**-lish
Is it free?	Ist es umsonst?	ist es oom-**zonst**

How much is it?	**Wieviel kostet das?**	vee-**feel** kos-tet dahs
Is the ticket good all day?	**Gilt die Karte den ganzen Tag lang?**	gilt dee **kar**-teh dayn **gahn**-tsen tahg lahng
Can I get back in?	**Kann ich wieder hinein?**	kahn ikh **vee**-der hin-**īn**
What time does this...?	**Um wieviel Uhr ist hier...?**	oom vee-**feel** oor ist heer
...open	**...geöffnet**	geh-**urf**-net
...close	**...geschlossen**	geh-**shlos**-sen
When is the last admission?	**Wann ist letzter Einlaß?**	vahn ist **lets**-ter **īn**-lahs
I beg of you, PLEASE let me in!	**BITTE, ich flehe Sie an, lassen Sie mich hinein!**	**bit**-teh ikh **flay**-heh zee ahn, **lah**-sen zee mikh hin-**īn**
I've traveled all the way from...	**Ich bin extra aus... gekommen.**	ikh bin **ehk**-strah ows... geh-**kom**-men
I must leave tomorrow.	**Ich muß morgen abreisen.**	ikh mus **mor**-gen **ahp**-rī-zen
I promise I'll be fast.	**Ich verspreche, mich zu beeilen.**	ikh fehr-**shprekh**-eh mikh tsoo **bay**-ī-len

Deciphering entrance signs:

Erwachsene	adults
Gesamtkarten	combo ticket
Führung	guided tour
Ausstellung	exhibit
Standort	you are here (on map)

Discounts:

You may be eligible for a discount at tourist sites, hotels, or on buses and trains—ask.

SIGHTSEEING

Is there a discount for...?	Gibt es Ermäßigung für...?	gipt es ehr-**may**-see-goong fewr
...youth	...Kinder	**kin**-der
...students	...Studenten	shtoo-**den**-ten
...families	...Familien	fah-**meel**-yen
...seniors	...Senioren	zen-**yor**-en
I am...	Ich bin...	ikh bin
He / She is...	Er / Sie ist...	ehr / zee ist
...___ years old.	...___ Jahre alt.	**yah**-reh ahlt

In the museum:

Where is...?	Wo ist...?	voh ist
I'd like to see...	Ich möchte gerne... sehen.	ikh **murkh**-teh **gehr**-neh... **zay**-hen
Photos / videos O.K.?	Fotografieren / filmen O.K.?	foh-toh-grah-**feer**-en / **fil**-men "O.K."
No flash.	Kein Blitz.	kīn blitz
No tripod.	Stativ verboten.	shtah-**teef** fehr-**boh**-ten
I like it.	Es gefällt mir.	es geh-**felt** meer
It's so...	Es ist so...	es ist zoh
...beautiful.	...schön.	shurn
...ugly.	...häßlich.	**hes**-likh
...strange.	...seltsam.	**zelt**-zahm
...boring.	...langweilig.	**lahng**-vī-lig
...interesting.	...interessant.	in-tehr-es-**sahnt**
Wow!	Fantastisch! Toll!	fahn-**tahs**-tish / tol
My feet have had it!	Meine Füße sind ganz plattgelaufen!	**mī**-neh **few**-seh zint gahnts **plaht**-geh-**lowf**-en
I'm exhausted!	Ich bin fertig!	ikh bin **fehr**-tig

Be careful when planning your sightseeing. Many museums close one day a week and many stop selling tickets 45 minutes or so before they close. Many sights are only shown to groups with a guide. Individuals usually end up with the next German escort. To get an English tour, call in advance to see if one's scheduled. Individuals can often tag along with a large tour group.

Art and architecture:

art	Kunst	kunst
artist	Künstler	**kewnst**-ler
painting	Gemälde	geh-**mayl**-deh
self portrait	Selbstporträt	**zelpst**-por-tray
sculptor	Bildhauer	**bilt**-how-er
sculpture	Skulptur	**skulp**-toor
architect	Architekt	**arkh**-i-tekt
architecture	Architektur	**arkh**-i-tek-toor
original	Original	oh-rig-ee-**nahl**
restored	restauriert	res-tow-**ree**-ert
B.C.	vor Christus (v. Chr.)	for **kris**-tus
A.D.	nach Christus (n. Chr.)	nahkh **kris**-tus
century	Jahrhundert	yar-**hoon**-dert
style	Stil	shteel
Abstract	Abstrakt	ahp-**strahkt**
Ancient	Altertümlich	**ahl**-ter-tewm-likh
Art Nouveaux	Jugendstil	**yoo**-gend-shteel
Baroque	Barock	bah-**rok**
Classical	Klassisch	**klah**-sish

Gothic	**Gothisch**	**goh**-tish
Impressionist	**Impressionistisch**	im-preh-see-oh-**nls**-tish
Medieval	**Mittelalterlich**	**mit**-tel-ahl-ter-likh
Modern	**Modern**	moh-**dehrn**
Neoclassical	**Neoklassizistisch**	**nay**-oh-klah-sits-is-tish
Renaissance	**Renaissance**	**ren**-ah-sahns
Romanesque	**Romanisch**	roh-**mahn**-ish
Romantic	**Romantik**	roh-**mahn**-tik

Castles and palaces:

castle	**Burg**	burg
palace	**Schloß**	shlos
kitchen	**Küche**	**kewkh**-en
hall	**Saal**	sahl
treasury	**Schatzkammer**	**shots**-kah-mer
cellar	**Keller**	**kel**-ler
dungeon	**Verlies**	**fehr**-lees
moat	**Burggraben**	**burg**-grah-ben
fortified wall	**Burgmauer**	**burg**-mow-er
tower	**Turm**	turm
fountain	**Brunnen**	**brun**-nen
garden	**Garten**	**gar**-ten
king	**König, Kaiser**	**kur**-nig, **kī**-zer
queen	**Königin**	**kur**-nig-in
knights	**Ritter**	**rit**-ter

You'll see the words *burg* (castle) and *berg* (mountain) linked to the end of names (such as Rothenburg and Ehrenberg). Salzburg means "salt-castle."

Religious words:

cathedral	**Kathedrale**	kah-tee-**drah**-leh
church	**Kirche**	**keerkh**-eh
monastery	**Kloster**	**klohs**-ter
synagogue	**Synagoge**	zin-ah-**goh**-geh
chapel	**Kapelle**	kah-**pel**-leh
altar	**Altar**	ahl-**tar**
cross	**Kreuz**	kroyts
crypt	**Krypte**	**krip**-teh
treasury	**Schatzkammer**	**shots**-kah-mer
dome	**Kuppel**	**kup**-pel
bells	**Glocken**	**glok**-en
organ	**Orgel**	**org**-el
relic	**Reliquie**	reh-**leek**-wee-eh
saint	**Heiliger**	**hī**-lig-er
God	**Gott**	got
Jewish	**jüdisch**	**yew**-dish
Moslem	**Moslem**	**moz**-lem
Christian	**christlich**	**krist**-likh
Protestant	**evangelisch**	eh-vahn-**gay**-lish
Catholic	**katholisch**	kah-**toh**-lish
agnostic	**agnostisch**	ahg-**nohs**-tish
atheist	**atheistisch**	ah-tay-**is**-tish
When is the service?	**Wann ist der Gottesdienst?**	vahn ist dehr **got**-tes-deenst
Are there church concerts?	**Gibt es Kirchen- konzerte?**	gipt es keerkh-en- kon-**tsehr**-teh

Shopping

Names of shops:

Where is a...?	Wo ist ein...?	voh ist īn
antique shop	Antiquitäten	ahn-tee-kwee-**tay**-ten
art gallery	Kunstgalerie	kunst-gah-leh-**ree**
bakery	Bäckerei	bek-eh-**rī**
barber shop	Herrenfrisör	hehr-ren-friz-**ur**
beauty salon	Damenfrisör	dah-men-friz-**ur**
book shop	Buchladen	**bookh**-lah-den
camera shop	Photoladen	**foh**-toh-lah-den
coffee shop	Kaffeeladen	kah-**fay**-lah-den
department store	Kaufhaus	**kowf**-hows
flea market	Flohmarkt	**floh**-markt
flower market	Blumenmarkt	**bloo**-men-markt
grocery store	Lebensmittelgeschäft	**lay**-bens-mit-tel-geh-**sheft**
hardware store	Eisenwarengeschäft	**ī**-zen-**vah**-ren-geh-**sheft**
jewelry shop	Schmuckladen	**shmuk**-lah-den
laundromat	Waschsalon	**vahsh**-zah-lon
newsstand	Zeitungsstand	**tsī**-toongs-shtahnt
office supplies	Bürobedarf	**bew**-roh-beh-darf
open air market	Markt	markt
optician	Optiker	**ohp**-ti-ker
pastry shop	Zuckerbäcker	**tsoo**-ker-bayk-er
pharmacy	Apotheke	ah-poh-**tay**-keh
photocopy shop	Kopierladen	**koh**-pee-ehr-lah-den
shopping mall	Einkaufszentrum	**īn**-kowfs-tsen-troom

souvenir shop	**Souvenir Shop**	"souvenir shop"
supermarket	**Supermarkt**	**zoo**-per-markt
toy store	**Spielzeugladen**	**shpeel**-tsoyg-lah-den
travel agency	**Reiseagentur**	**rī**-zeh-ah-gen-tur
used bookstore	**Bücher aus zweiter Hand, Antiquariat**	**bookh**-er ows tsvī-ter hahnd, ahn-tee-**kwah**-ree-aht
wine shop	**Weinhandlung**	**vīn**-hahnt-loong

Many businesses close from 12:00 to 15:00 on weekday afternoons and all day on Sundays. Typical hours are Monday through Friday 9:00 to 18:00, Saturday 9:00 to 13:00. Some stores stay open Thursdays until 21:00.

Shop till you drop:

opening hours	**Öffnungszeiten**	urf-noongs-**tsī**-ten
sale	**Ausverkauf**	**ows**-fehr-kowf
special	**Angebot**	**ahn**-geh-boht
good value	**preiswert**	**prīs**-vehrt
How much is it?	**Wieviel kostet das?**	vee-**feel kos**-tet dahs
I'm just browsing.	**Ich sehe mich nur um.**	ikh **zay**-heh mikh noor oom
We're just browsing.	**Wir sehen uns nur um.**	veer **zay**-hen uns noor oom
Where can I buy...?	**Wo kann ich kaufen...?**	voh kahn ikh **kow**-fen
I'd like...	**Ich möchte...**	ikh **murkh**-teh
Do you have...?	**Haben Sie...?**	**hah**-ben zee
...more	**...mehr**	mehr
...something cheaper	**...etwas billigeres**	**et**-vahs **bil**-lig-er-es

...better quality	...bessere Qualität	**bes**-ser-er **kwah**-lee-tayt
This one.	Dieses.	**dee**-zes
Can I try it on?	Kann ich es anprobieren?	kahn ikh es **ahn**-proh-beer-en
Do you have a mirror?	Haben Sie einen Spiegel?	**hah**-ben zee ī-nen **shpee**-gel
Too...	Zu...	tsoo
...big.	...groß.	grohs
...small.	...klein.	klīn
...expensive.	...teuer.	**toy**-er
Did you make this?	Haben Sie das gemacht?	**hah**-ben zee dahs geh-**mahkht**
What is it made out of?	Was ist das für Material?	vahs ist dahs fewr mah-ter-ee-**ahl**
Machine washable?	Waschmaschinenfest?	**vahsh**-mah-sheen-en-fest
Will it shrink?	Läuft es ein?	loyft es īn
Credit card O.K.?	Kreditkarte O.K.?	kreh-**deet**-kar-teh "O.K."
Can you ship this?	Können Sie das versenden?	**kurn**-nen zee dahs fehr-**zen**-den
Tax-free?	Steuerfrei?	**shtoy**-er-frī
I'll think about it.	Ich denk drüber nach.	ikh denk **drew**-ber nahkh
What time do you close?	Um wieviel Uhr schließen Sie?	oom vee-**feel** oor **shlee**-sen zee
What time do you open tomorrow?	Wann öffnen Sie morgen?	vahn **urf**-nen zee **mor**-gen
Is that your lowest price?	Ist das der günstigste Preis?	ist dahs dehr **gewn**-stig-steh prīs
My last offer.	Mein letztes Angebot.	mīn **lets**-tes **ahn**-geh-boht

Good price.	**Guter Preis.**	goo-ter prīs
I'll take it.	**Ich nehme es.**	ikh **nay**-meh es
I'm nearly broke.	**Ich bin fast pleite.**	ikh bin fahst **plī**-teh
My male friend...	**Mein Freund...**	mīn froynd
My female friend...	**Meine Freundin...**	**mī**-neh **froyn**-din
My husband...	**Mein Mann...**	mīn mahn
My wife...	**Meine Frau...**	**mī**-neh frow
...has the money.	**...hat das Geld.**	haht dahs gelt

For colors and fabrics, see the dictionary near the end of this book.

Repair:

These handy lines can apply to any repair, whether it's a cranky zipper, broken leg, or dying car.

This is broken.	**Das hier ist kaputt.**	dahs heer ist kah-**put**
Can you fix it?	**Können Sie das reparieren?**	**kurn**-nen zee dahs reh-pah-**reer**-en
Just do the essentials.	**Machen Sie nur das Nötigste.**	**mahkh**-en zee noor dahs **nur**-tig-steh
How much will it cost?	**Wieviel kostet das?**	vee-**feel** **kos**-tet dahs
When will it be ready?	**Wann ist es fertig?**	vahn ist es **fehr**-tig
I need it by ___.	**Ich brauche es um ___.**	ikh **browkh**-eh es oom

SHOPPING

Entertainment

What's happening tonight?	**Was ist heute abend los?**	vahs ist **hoy**-teh **ah**-bent lohs
Can you recommend something?	**Können Sie etwas empfehlen?**	**kurn**-nen zee **et**-vahs emp-**fay**-len
Is it free?	**Ist es umsonst?**	ist es oom-**zohnst**
Where can I buy a ticket?	**Wo kann ich eine Karte kaufen?**	voh kahn ikh **ī**-neh **kar**-teh **kowf**-en
When does it start?	**Wann fängt es an?**	vahn fengt es ahn
When does it end?	**Wann endet es?**	vahn **en**-det es
Will you go out with me?	**Möchten Sie mit mir ausgehen?**	**murkh**-ten zee mit meer **ows**-gay-hen
Where's the best place to dance nearby?	**Wo geht man hier am besten tanzen?**	voh gayt mahn heer ahm **bes**-ten **tahn**-tsen
Do you want to dance?	**Möchten Sie tanzen?**	**murkh**-ten zee **tahn**-tsen
Again?	**Noch einmal?**	nokh **īn**-mahl
Let's party!	**Feiern wir!**	**fī**-ern veer

What's happening:

movie...	**Film...**	film
...original version	**...im Original**	im oh-rig-ee-**nahl**
...in English	**...auf englisch**	owf **eng**-lish
...with subtitles	**...mit Untertiteln**	mit **oon**-ter-tee-teln
...dubbed	**...übersetzt**	ew-behr-**zetst**
music...	**Musik...**	moo-**zeek**
...live	**...live**	"live"

...classical	**...klassisch**	**klahs**-sish
folk music	**Volksmusik**	**fohlks**-moo-zeek
old rock	**Alter Rock**	**ahl**-ter rok
jazz	**Jazz**	"jazz"
blues	**Blues**	"blues"
singer	**Sänger**	**zeng**-er
concert	**Konzert**	kon-**tsert**
show	**Vorführung**	for-few-roong
dancing	**Tanzen**	**tahn**-tsen
folk dancing	**Folkstanz**	**fohlks**-tahnts
disco	**Disko**	**dis**-koh
cover charge	**Eintritt**	**în**-trit

Oktoberfest, the famous Munich beer festival, fills Bavaria's capital with the sounds of *"Prost!"*, carnival rides, sizzling bratwurst, and oompah bands. The party starts the third Saturday in September and lasts for 16 days. The *Salzburger Festspiele* (Salzburg's music festival) gives visitors the sound of music from late July to the end of August. Each country's national tourist office in the U.S.A. can mail you a free schedule (in English) of upcoming festivals.

ENTERTAINMENT

Phoning

Where is the nearest phone?	Wo ist das nächste Telefon?	voh ist dahs nekh-steh tel-eh-fohn
I'd like to telephone...	Ich möchte einen Anruf nach... machen.	ikh murkh-teh ī-nen ahn-roof nahkh... mahkh-en
...the U.S.A.	...U.S.A.	oo es ah
What is the cost per minute?	Wieviel kostet es pro Minute?	vee-feel kos-tet es proh mee-noo-teh
I'd like to make a... call.	Ich möchte ein... machen.	ikh murkh-teh īn... mahkh-en
...local	...Ortsgespräch	orts-geh-shpraykh
...collect	...R-gespräch	ehr-geh-shpraykh
...credit card	...Kreditkarten- gespräch	kreh-deet-kar-ten- geh-shpraykh
...long distance	...Ferngespräch	fehrn-geh-shpraykh
It doesn't work.	Es außer Betrieb.	es ow-ser beh-treep
May I use your phone?	Darf ich mal Ihr Telefon benutzen?	darf ikh mahl eer tel-eh-fohn beh-noo-tsen
Can you dial for me?	Können Sie für mich wählen?	kurn-nen zee fewr mikh vay-len
Can you talk for me?	Können Sie für mich sprechen?	kurn-nen zee fewr mikh shprekh-en
It's busy.	Besetzt.	beh-zetst
Will you try again?	Noch einmal versuchen?	nokh īn-mahl fehr-zookh-en
Hello? (on phone)	Ja, bitte?	yah bit-teh
My name is...	Ich heiße...	ikh hī-seh
My number is...	Meine Telefon- nummer ist...	mī-neh tel-eh-fohn- num-mer ist

Speak slowly.	**Sprechen Sie langsam.**	shprekh-en zee lahng-zahm
Wait a moment.	**Moment.**	moh-**ment**
Don't hang up.	**Nicht auflegen.**	nikht **owf**-lay-gen

Key telephone words:

telephone	**Telefon**	tel-eh-**fohn**
telephone card	**Telefonkarte**	tel-eh-**fohn**-kar-teh
operator	**Vermittlung**	fehr-**mit**-loong
international assistance	**Internationale Auskunft**	in-tehr-naht-see-oh-**nah**-leh **ows**-koonft
country code	**Landesvorwahl**	**lahn**-des-for-vahl
area code	**Vorwahl**	**for**-vahl
telephone book	**Telefonbuch**	tel-eh-**fohn**-bookh
yellow pages	**Gelbe Seiten**	**gehlp**-eh **zi**-ten
toll-free	**gebührenfrei**	geh-**bew**-ren-fri
out of service	**Außer Betrieb**	**ow**-ser beh-**treep**

In Germany, it's considered polite to identify yourself by name at the beginning of every phone conversation. A telephone card (*Telefonkarte*), available at post offices and newsstands, is handier than using coins for your calls. Post offices also have easy-to-use metered phones.

At phone booths, you'll encounter these words: *Kartentelefon* (accepts cards, sometimes coins as well), *Ganzeinschieben* (insert completely), *Bitte wählen* (please dial), and *Guthaben* (the amount of money left on your card). If the number you're calling is out of service, you'll hear the dreaded recording: *"Kein Anschluss unter dieser Nummer."* For more tips, see "Let's Talk Telephones."

E-mail

e-mail	**e-mail**	**ee**-mayl
internet	**Internet**	**in**-tehr-net
May I please check my e-mail?	**Kann ich mein e-mail nachlesen, bitte?**	kahn ikh mīn **ee**-mayl **nahkh**-lay-zen **bit**-teh
Where can I get access to the internet?	**Wo gibt es einen Internet Zugang, bitte?**	voh gipt es **ī**-nen **in**-tehr-net **tsoo**-ghang **bit**-teh
Where is the nearest cybercafé?	**Wo ist das nächste Internet Café?**	voh ist dahs **naykh**-steh **in**-tehr-net kah-**fay**

On the computer screen:

Ansicht	view	**öffnen**	open
bearbeiten	edit	**Ordner**	file
drucken	print	**Post**	mail
löschen	delete	**senden**	send
Mitteilung	message	**speichern**	save

Post Office

Where is the post office?	**Wo ist die Post?**	voh ist dee post
Which window for...?	**An welchem Schalter ist...?**	ahn **vehlkh**-em **shahl**-ter ist
Is this the line for...?	**Ist das die Schlange für...?**	ist dahs dee **shlahn**-geh fewr
...stamps	**...Briefmarken**	**breef**-mar-ken

...packages	**...Pakete**	pah-**kay**-teh
To America....	**Nach Amerika...**	nahkh ah-**mehr**-ee-kah
...by air mail.	**...mit Luftpost.**	mit **luft**-post
...slow and cheap.	**...langsam und billig.**	**lahng**-zahm oont **bil**-lig
How much is it?	**Wieviel kostet das?**	vee-**feel kos**-tet dahs
How many days will it take?	**Wieviele Tage braucht das?**	vee-**fee**-leh **tahg**-eh browkht dahs

Licking the postal code:

German	**Deutsche**	**doy**-cheh
Postal Service	**Bundespost**	**boon**-des-post
post office	**Postamt**	**post**-ahmt
stamp	**Briefmarke**	**breef**-mar-keh
postcard	**Postkarte**	**post**-kar-teh
letter	**Brief**	breef
aerogram	**Luftpostpapier**	**luft**-post-pah-**peer**
envelope	**Umschlag**	**oom**-shlahg
package	**Paket**	pah-**kayt**
box	**Karton**	kar-**ton**
string	**Schnur**	shnoor
tape	**Klebeband**	**klay**-beh-bahnd
mailbox	**Briefkasten**	**breef**-kahs-ten
air mail	**Luftpost**	**luft**-post
express mail	**Eilpost**	**il**-post
slow and cheap	**langsam und billig**	**lahng**-zahm oont **bil**-lig
book rate	**Büchersendung**	**bewkh**-er-**zayn**-doong
weight limit	**Gewichtsbegren- zung**	geh-**vikhts**-beh-gren- tsoong
registered	**Einschreiben**	**in**-shri-ben

insured	**versichert**	fehr-**zikh**-ert
fragile	**zerbrechlich**	tsehr-**brekh**-likh
contents	**Inhalt**	**in**-hahlt
customs	**Zoll**	tsol
to	**nach**	nahkh
from	**von**	fon
address	**Adresse**	ah-**dres**-seh
zip code	**Postleitzahl**	**post**-līt-sahl
general delivery	**postlagernd**	**post**-lah-gehrnt

In Germany, Austria, and Switzerland, you can often get stamps at the corner *Tabakladen* (tobacco shop). As long as you know which stamps you need, this is a great convenience. At the post office, the window labeled "Alle Leistungen" handles everything.

To save money, mail your postcards outside of Germany. If mailing a package from Germany, consider *Economy Plus*. It's slower and cheaper than air mail, and faster than surface mail. German mail boxes often come in pairs: the box for local mail is labeled with its range of zip codes, and the other box (labeled *Andere PLZ*) is for everything else.

Red Tape & Profanity

Filling out forms:

Herr / Frau / Fräulein	Mr. / Mrs. / Miss
Vorname	first name
Name	name
Adresse	address
Wohnort	address
Straße	street
Stadt	city
Staat	state
Land	country
Nationalität	nationality
Herkunft / Reiseziel	origin / destination
Alter	age
Geburtsdatum	date of birth
Geburtsort	place of birth
Geschlecht	sex
männlich / weiblich	male / female
verheiratet / ledig	married / single
Beruf	profession
Erwachsener	adult
Kind / Junge / Mädchen	child / boy / girl
Kinder	children
Familie	family
Unterschrift	signature

RED TAPE

When filling out dates, do it European-style:
day/month/year (Christmas is 25/12/01).

German profanity:

In any country, red tape can lead to a blue streak. These words will help you understand what the more colorful locals are saying...

Damn it.	**Verdammt.**	fehr-**dahmt**
Shit.	**Scheiße.**	**shī**-seh
Go to hell.	**Geh zur Hölle.**	gay tsur **hurl**-leh
Screw it.	**Scheiß drauf.**	**shīs** drowf
Sit on it.	**Am Arsch.**	ahm arsh
bastard (pig-dog)	**Schweinehund**	**shvī**-neh-hoont
bitch (goat)	**Ziege**	**tsee**-geh
breasts (colloq.)	**Titten**	**tit**-en
penis (colloq.)	**Schwanz**	shvahnts
butthole	**Arschloch**	**arsh**-lokh
drunk	**besoffen**	beh-**zof**-fen
stupid (dumb head)	**Dummkopf**	**dum**-kopf
Did someone fart?	**Hat jemand gefurzt?**	haht **yay**-mahnd geh-**furtst**
I burped.	**Ich habe gerülpst.**	ikh **hah**-beh geh-**rewlpst**

Help!

Help!	**Hilfe!**	**hil**-feh
Help me!	**Helfen Sie mir!**	**hel**-fen zee meer
Call a doctor!	**Rufen Sie einen Arzt!**	**roo**-fen zee **ī**-nen artst
ambulance	**Krankenwagen**	**krahn**-ken-vah-gen
accident	**Unfall**	**oon**-fahl
injured	**verletzt**	fehr-**letst**
emergency	**Notfall**	**noht**-fahl
police	**Polizei**	poh-leet-**sī**
thief	**Dieb**	deep
pick-pocket	**Taschendieb**	**tahsh**-en-deep
I've been ripped off.	**Ich bin bestohlen worden.**	ikh bin beh-**shtoh**-len **vor**-den
I've lost my...	**Ich habe meine... verloren.**	ikh **hah**-beh **mī**-neh... fehr-**lor**-en
...passport.	**...Paß**	pahs
...ticket.	**...Karte**	**kar**-teh
...baggage.	**...Gepäck**	geh-**pek**
...purse.	**...Handtasche**	**hahnd**-tash-eh
...wallet.	**...Brieftasche**	**breef**-tash-eh
...faith in humankind.	**...Glauben an die Menschheit**	**glow**-ben ahn dee **mehnsh**-hīt
I'm lost.	**Ich habe mich verlaufen.**	ikh **hah**-beh mikh fehr-**lowf**-en

HELP!

Help for women:

Leave me alone.	**Lassen Sie mich in Ruhe.**	**lah**-sen zee mikh in **roo**-heh
I *vant* to be alone.	**Ich möchte alleine sein.**	ikh **murkh**-teh ah-**lī**-neh zīn
I'm not interested.	**Ich hab kein Interesse.**	ikh hahp kīn in-tehr-**es**-seh
I'm married.	**Ich bin verheiratet.**	ikh bin fehr-**hī**-rah-tet
I'm a lesbian.	**Ich bin lesbisch.**	ikh bin **lez**-bish
I have a contagious disease.	**Ich habe eine ansteckende Krankheit.**	ikh **hah**-beh ī-neh **ahn**-shtek-en-deh **krahnk**-hīt
You are intrusive.	**Sie sind aufdringlich.**	zee zint **owf**-dring-likh
This man is bothering me.	**Der Mann stört mich.**	dehr mahn shturt mikh
Don't touch me.	**Fassen Sie mich nicht an.**	**fah**-sen zee mikh nikht ahn
You're disgusting.	**Sie sind eklig.**	zee zint **ek**-lig
Stop following me.	**Hör auf, mir nachzulaufen.**	hur owf meer **nahkh**-tsoo-**lowf**-en
Enough!	**Das reicht!**	dahs rīkht
Go away.	**Gehen Sie weg.**	**gay**-en zee vayg
Get lost!	**Hau ab!**	how ahp
Drop dead!	**Verschwinde!**	fehr-**shvin**-deh
I'll call the police.	**Ich rufe die Polizei.**	ikh **roo**-feh dee poh-leet-**sī**

Health

I feel sick.	**Mir ist schlecht.**	meer ist shlekht
I need a doctor...	**Ich brauche einen Arzt...**	ikh **browkh**-eh **ī**-nen artst
...who speaks English.	**...der Englisch spricht.**	dehr **eng**-lish shprikht
It hurts here.	**Hier tut es weh.**	heer toot es vay
I'm allergic to...	**Ich bin allergisch gegen...**	ikh bin ah-**lehr**-gish **gay**-gen
...penicillin.	**...Penizillin.**	pen-ee-tsee-**leen**
I am diabetic.	**Ich bin Diabetiker.**	ikh bin dee-ah-**bet**-ee-ker
I've missed a period.	**Ich habe meine Tage nicht bekommen.**	ikh **hah**-beh **mī**-neh **tahg**-eh nikht beh-**kom**-men
My male friend has...	**Mein Freund hat...**	mīn froynd haht
My female friend has...	**Meine Freundin hat...**	**mī**-neh **froyn**-din haht
I have...	**Ich habe...**	ikh **hah**-beh
...asthma.	**...Asthma.**	**ahst**-mah
...athelete's foot.	**...Fusspilz.**	**foos**-pilts
...a burn.	**...eine Verbrennung.**	**ī**-neh fehr-**bren**-noong
...chest pains.	**...Schmerzen in der Brust.**	**shmehrt**-sen in dehr brust
...a cold.	**...eine Erkältung.**	**ī**-neh ehr-**kel**-toong
...constipation.	**...Verstopfung.**	fehr-**shtop**-foong
...a cough.	**...einen Husten.**	**ī**-nen **hoo**-sten
...diarrhea.	**...Durchfall.**	**durkh**-fahl
...dizziness.	**...Schwindel.**	**shvin**-del
...a fever.	**...Fieber.**	**fee**-ber
...the flu.	**...die Grippe.**	dee **grip**-peh
...giggles.	**...einen Lachanfall.**	**ī**-nen **lahkh**-ahn-fahl

...hay fever.	...Heuschnupfen.	**hoysh**-nup-fen
...a headache.	...Kopfschmerzen.	**kopf**-shmehrt-sen
...hemorrhoids.	...Hämorrholden.	hay-mor-**hohl**-den
...high blood pressure.	...Bluthochdruck.	**bloot**-hokh-druk
...indigestion.	...Verdauungsstörung.	fehr-**dow**-oongs-shtur-oong
...an infection.	...eine Entzündung.	**ī**-neh ent-**sewn**-doong
...insect bites.	...Insektenstiche.	in-zek-ten-**shtikh**-eh
...a migraine.	...Migräne.	mee-**gray**-neh
...nausea.	...Übelkeit.	**ew**-bel-kīt
...a rash.	...einen Ausschlag.	**ī**-nen **ows**-shlahg
...a sore throat.	...Halsschmerzen.	**hahls**-shmehrt-sen
...a stomach ache.	...Magenschmerzen.	**mah**-gen-shmehrt-sen
...a swelling.	...eine Schwellung.	**ī**-neh **shvel**-loong
...a toothache.	...Zahnschmerzen.	**tsahn**-shmehrt-sen
...urinary infection.	...Harnröhrenentzündung.	**harn**-rur-ren-ent-tsewn-doong
...a venereal disease.	...eine Geschlechtskrankeit.	**ī**-neh geh-**shlekhts**-krahn-kīt
...worms.	...Würmer.	**vewr**-mer
I have body odor.	Ich habe Körpergeruch.	ikh **hah**-beh **kur**-per-geh-rookh
Is it serious?	Ist es ernst?	ist es ehrnst

Handy health words:

pain	Schmerz	shmehrts
dentist	Zahnarzt	**tsahn**-artst
doctor	Arzt	artst
nurse	Krankenschwester	**krahn**-ken-shves-ter

health insurance	**Krankenversicherung**	krahn-ken-fehr-**zikh**-eh-roong
hospital	**Krankenhaus**	**krahn**-ken-hows
blood	**Blut**	bloot
bandage	**Verband**	fehr-**bahnt**
medicine	**Medikamente**	med-ee-kah-**men**-teh
pharmacy	**Apotheke**	ah-poh-**tay**-keh
prescription	**Rezept**	reh-**tsehpt**
pill	**Pille**	**pil**-leh
aspirin	**Aspirin**	ah-spir-**een**
non-aspirin substitute	**Ben-u-ron**	**behn**-oo-ron
antibiotic	**Antibiotika**	ahn-tee-bee-**oh**-tee-kah
cold medicine	**Grippemittel**	**grip**-eh-mit-tel
cough drops	**Hustenbonbons**	**hoo**-sten-bohn-bohz
antacid	**Mittel gegen Magenbrennen**	**mit**-tel **gay**-gen **mah**-gen-bren-nen
pain killer	**Schmerzmittel**	**shmehrts**-mit-tel
Preparation H	**Hemorrihden Salbe**	hem-oh-**rid**-den **zahl**-beh
vitamins	**Vitamine**	**vee**-tah-mee-neh

Glasses and contact lenses:

glasses	**Brille**	**bril**-leh
sunglasses	**Sonnenbrille**	**zoh**-nen-bril-leh
prescription	**Rezept**	reh-**tsept**
soft lenses	**Weiche Linsen**	**vīkh**-eh lin-zen
hard lenses	**Harte Linsen**	**har**-teh lin-zen
cleaning solution	**Reinigungslösung**	**rī**-nee-goongs-lur-zoong
soaking solution	**Kontaktlinsenbad**	kon-**tahkt**-lin-zen-baht
I've... a contact lens.	**Ich habe meine Kontaktlinse...**	ikh **hah**-beh **mī**-neh kon-**tahkt**-lin-zeh
...lost	**...verloren.**	fehr-**lor**-en
...swallowed	**...verschluckt.**	fehr-**shlukt**

Toiletries:

comb	**Kamm**	kahm
conditioner	**Spülung**	**shpew**-loong
condoms	**Kondome**	**kohn**-doh-meh
dental floss	**Zahnseide**	**tsahn**-zī-deh
deodorant	**Deodorant**	deh-oh-doh-**rahnt**
hairbrush	**Haarbürste**	**har**-bewr-steh
hand lotion	**Handcreme**	**hahnd**-kreh-meh
lip salve	**Lippenpflege**	**lip**-pen-fleg-eh
nail clipper	**Nagelschere**	**nahg**-el-sheh-reh
razor	**Rasierer**	rah-**zeer**-er
sanitary napkins	**Damenbinden**	**dah**-men-bin-den
shampoo	**Shampoo**	**shahm**-poo
shaving cream	**Rasierseife**	rah-**zeer**-zī-feh
soap	**Seife**	**zī**-feh
sunscreen	**Sonnencreme**	**zoh**-nen-kreh-meh
tampons	**Tampons**	**tahm**-pohnz
tissues	**Taschentücher**	**tah**-shen-tewkh-er
toilet paper	**Klopapier**	kloh-pah-**peer**
toothbrush	**Zahnbürste**	**tsahn**-bewr-steh
toothpaste	**Zahnpasta**	**tsahn**-pah-stah
tweezers	**Pinzette**	pin-**tseh**-teh

Chatting

My name is...	**Ich heiße...**	ikh **hī**-seh
What's your name?	**Wie heißen Sie?**	vee **hī**-sen zee
This is...	**Das ist...**	dahs ist
How are you?	**Wie geht's?**	vee gayts
Very well, thanks.	**Sehr gut, danke.**	zehr goot **dahng**-keh
Where are you from?	**Woher kommen Sie?**	**voh**-hehr **kom**-men zee
What...?	**Von welcher...?**	fon **velkh**-er
...city	**...Stadt**	shtaht
...country	**...Land**	lahnd
...planet	**...Planet**	plahn-**et**
I'm from...	**Ich bin aus...**	ikh bin ows
...America.	**...Amerika.**	ah-**mehr**-i-kah
...Canada.	**...Kanada.**	**kah**-nah-dah

Nothing more than feelings...

I am / You are...	**Ich bin / Sie sind...**	ikh bin / zee zint
...happy.	**...glücklich.**	glewk-likh
...sad.	**...traurig.**	**trow**-rig
...tired.	**...müde.**	**mew**-deh
...hungry.	**...hungrig.**	**hoon**-grig
...thirsty.	**...durstig.**	**dur**-stig
I'm cold.	**Mir ist kalt.**	meer ist kahlt
I'm too warm.	**Mir ist zu warm.**	meer ist tsoo varm
I'm homesick.	**Ich habe Heimweh.**	ikh **hah**-beh **hīm**-vay
I'm lucky.	**Ich habe Glück.**	ikh **hah**-beh glewk

Who's who:

This is a... of mine.	Das ist...von mir.	dahs ist in... fon meer
...male friend	...ein Freund	in froynd
...female friend	...eine Freundin	i-neh **froyn**-din
My...	Mein / meine...	min / **mi**-neh
...boyfriend / girlfriend.	...Freund / Freundin.	froynd / **froyn**-din
...husband / wife.	...Mann / Frau.	mahn / frow
...son / daughter.	...Sohn / Tochter.	zohn / **tokh**-ter
...brother / sister.	...Bruder / Schwester.	**broo**-der / **shves**-ter
...father / mother.	...Vater / Mutter.	**fah**-ter / **mut**-ter
...uncle / aunt.	...Onkel / Tante.	**ohn**-kel / **tahn**-teh
...nephew / niece.	...Neffe / Nichte.	**nef**-feh / **neekh**-teh
...male / female cousin.	...Cousin / Cousine.	koo-**zeen** / koo-**zee**-neh
...grandfather / grandmother.	...Großvater / Großmutter.	**grohs**-fah-ter / **grohs**-mut-ter
...grandson / granddaughter.	...Enkel / Enkelin.	**en**-kel / **en**-kel-in

Family and work:

Are you married?	Sind Sie verheiratet?	zint zee fehr-**hi**-rah-tet
Do you have children?	Haben Sie Kinder?	**hah**-ben zee **kin**-der
How many boys / girls?	Wieviele Jungen / Mädchen?	vee-**fee**-leh **yoong**-gen / **mayd**-khen
Do you have photos?	Haben Sie Fotos?	**hah**-ben zee **foh**-tohs
How old is your child?	Wie alt ist Ihr Kind?	vee ahlt ist eer kint
Beautiful child!	Schönes Kind!	**shur**-nes kint
Beautiful children!	Schöne Kinder!	**shur**-neh **kin**-der

What is your occupation?	**Was machen Sie beruflich?**	vahs **mahkh**-en zee beh-**roof**-likh
Do you like your work?	**Gefällt Ihnen ihre Arbeit?**	geh-**felt ee**-nen **eer**-eh ar-bĭt
I'm a...	**Ich bin...**	ikh bin
...student. (male / female)	...**Student / Studentin.**	shtoo-**dent** / shtoo-**dent**-in
...teacher. (male / female)	...**Lehrer / Lehrerin.**	**lehr**-er / **lehr**-er-in
...worker.	...**Arbeiter.**	**ar**-bĭ-ter
...bureaucrat.	...**Bürokrat.**	**bew**-roh-kraht
...professional traveler.	...**professioneller Reisender.**	proh-fes-see-ohn-**nel**-ler **rī**-zen-der
Can I please take a photo of you?	**Darf ich ein Foto von Ihnen machen, bitte?**	darf ikh īn **foh**-toh fon **ee**-nen **mahkh**-en **bit**-teh

Chatting with children:

What's your name?	**Wie heist Du?**	vee hīst doo
My name is...	**Ich heiße...**	ikh **hī**-seh
How old are you?	**Wie alt bist Du?**	vee ahlt bist doo
Do you have siblings?	**Hast Du Geschwister?**	hahst doo geh-**shvis**-ter
Do you like school?	**Magst Du die Schule?**	mahgst doo dee **shoo**-leh
What are you studying?	**Was studierst Du?**	vahs shtoo-**deerst** doo
I'm studying...	**Ich studiere...**	ikh shtoo-**deer**-eh
What's your favorite subject?	**Was ist Dein Lieblingsfach?**	vahs ist dīn **lee**-blings-fahkh
Do you have pets?	**Hast Du Haustiere?**	hahst doo **how**-stee-ehr

CHATTING

...cat / dog / fish	...Katze / Hund / Fische	kaht-tseh / hoont / fish-eh
I have...	Ich habe...	ikh hah-beh
Will you please teach me some German words?	Bringst Du mir bitte einige deutsche Wörter bei?	bringst doo meer bit-teh ī-nig-eh doy-cheh vur-ter bī
What is this?	Was ist das?	vahs ist dahs
Will you teach me a simple German song?	Kannst Du mir ein einfaches deutsches Lied beibringen?	kahnst doo meer īn īn-fahkh-es doy-ches leet bī-bring-gen
Guess which country I live in.	Rate mal, in welchem Land ich wohne.	rah-teh mahl in velkh-em lahnt ikh voh-neh
How old am I?	Wie alt bin ich?	vee ahlt bin ikh
I'm ___ years old.	Ich bin ___ Jahre alt.	ikh bin ___ yah-reh ahlt
Want to thumb-wrestle?	Willst Du Daumenziehen?	vilst doo dow-men-tsee-hen
Want to hear me burp?	Willst Du meinen Rülpser hören?	vilst doo mī-nen rewlp-zer hur-en
Teach me a fun game.	Bringe mir ein lustiges Spiel bei.	bring-eh meer īn loo-shtig-es shpeel bī
Got any candy?	Hast Du Süssigkeiten?	hahst doo sew-sig-kī-ten

Travel talk:

I am / Are you...?	**Ich bin / Sind Sie...?**	ikh bin / zint zee
...on vacation	**...auf Urlaub**	owf **oor**-lowp
Are you working today?	**Arbeiten Sie heute?**	ar-**bīt**-en zee **hoy**-teh
How long have you been traveling?	**Wie lange sind Sie schon im Urlaub?**	vee **lahng**-eh zint zee shohn im **oor**-lowp
day / week / month / year	**Tag / Woche / Monat / Jahr**	tahg / **vokh**-eh / **moh**-naht / yar
When are you going home?	**Wann fahren Sie zurück?**	vahn **far**-en zee tsoo-**rewk**
This is my first time in...	**Ich bin zum ersten Mal in...**	ikh bin tsoom **ehr**-sten mahl in
It's (not) a tourist trap.	**Es ist (nicht) nur für Touristen.**	es ist (nikht) noor fewr too-**ris**-ten
Today / Tomorrow I'm going to...	**Heute / Morgen fahre ich nach...**	**hoy**-teh / **mor**-gen **far**-eh ikh nahkh
I'm very happy here.	**Ich bin sehr glücklich hier.**	ikh bin zehr **glewk**-likh heer
This is paradise.	**Das ist das Paradies.**	dahs ist dahs **pah**-rah-dees
The Germans / Austrians / Swiss...	**Die Deutschen / Österreicher / Schweizer...**	dee **doy**-chen / **urs**-teh-rīkh-er / **shvīt**-ser
...are very friendly.	**...sind sehr freundlich.**	zint zehr **froynd**-likh
This is a wonderful country.	**Dies ist ein wunderbares Land.**	deez ist īn **voon**-dehr-bah-res lahnd
Travel is good living.	**Auf Reisen lebt's sich gut.**	owf **rī**-zen laypts zikh goot
Have a good trip!	**Gute Reise!**	**goo**-teh **rī**-zeh

Map talk:

These phrases and maps will help you delve into family history and explore travel dreams.

I live here.	**Ich wohne hier.**	ikh **voh**-neh heer
I was born here.	**Ich bin hier geboren.**	ikh bin heer geh-**boh**-ren
My ancestors came from...	**Meine Vorfahren kamen aus...**	**mī**-neh for-far-en **kah**-men ows
I've traveled to...	**Ich bin hier gewesen...**	ikh bin heer geh-**vay**-zen
Next I'll go to...	**Als nächstes gehe ich nach...**	als **nekh**-stes **gay**-heh ikh nahkh
Where do you live?	**Wo wohnen Sie?**	voh **voh**-nen zee
Where were you born?	**Wo sind Sie geboren?**	voh zint zee geh-**boh**-ren
Where did your ancestors come from?	**Woher kommen ihre Vorfahren?**	**voh**-hehr **kom**-men ee-reh for-far-en
Where have you traveled?	**Wo sind Sie schon gewesen?**	voh zint zee shohn geh-**vay**-zen
Where are you going?	**Wohin gehen Sie?**	**voh**-hin **gay**-hen zee
Where would you like to go?	**Wohin möchten Sie?**	**voh**-hin **murkh**-ten zee

Germany

Austria

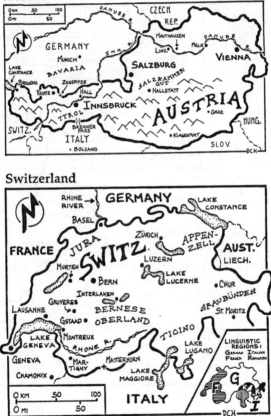

Switzerland

Weather:

What's the weather tomorrow?	**Wie wird das Wetter morgen?**	vee virt dahs **veht**-ter **mor**-gen
sunny / cloudy	**sonnig / bewölkt**	**zon**-nig / beh-**vurlkt**
hot / cold	**heiß / kalt**	hīs / kahlt
muggy / windy	**schwül / windig**	shvewl / **vin**-dig
rain / snow	**Regen / Schnee**	**ray**-gen / shnay

Favorite things:

What is your favorite...?	**Was ist Ihr Lieblings...?**	vahs ist eer **lee**-bleengs
...art	**...Kunst**	kunst
...artist	**...Künstler**	**kewnst**-ler
...author	**...Autor**	**ow**-tor
...book	**...Buch**	bookh
...music	**...Musik**	moo-**zeek**
...singer	**...Sänger**	**zeng**-er
...movie	**...Film**	"film"
...movie star	**...Filmstar**	"filmstar"
...food	**...Essen**	**es**-sen
...ice cream	**...Eis**	īs
...hobby	**...Hobby**	"hobby"
...sport	**...Sport**	shport
...vice	**...Sünde**	**zewn**-deh

Responses for all occasions:

I like that.	Das gefällt mir.	dahs geh-**felt** meer
I like you.	Sie gefallen mir.	zee geh-**fah**-len meer
That's cool!	Hey, cool!	"hey, cool"
Excellent!	Ausgezeichnet!	ows-get-**sīkh**-net
What a nice place.	Was für ein herrlicher Ort.	vahs fewr īn **hehr**-likh-er ort
Perfect.	Perfekt.	per-**fekt**
Funny.	Komisch.	**koh**-mish
Interesting.	Interessant.	in-tehr-es-**sahnt**
I don't smoke.	Ich rauche nicht.	ikh **rowkh**-eh nikht
I haven't any.	Ich habe keine.	ikh **hah**-beh kī-neh
Really?	Wirklich?	**virk**-likh
Congratulations!	Herzlichen Glückwunsch!	**hehrts**-likh-en **glewk**-vunsh
Well done!	Gut gemacht!	goot geh-**mahkht**
You're welcome.	Bitte schön.	**bit**-teh shurn
Bless you! (after sneeze)	Gesundheit!	geh-**zoond**-hīt
Excuse me.	Entschuldigung.	ent-**shool**-dee-goong
What a pity.	Wie schade.	vee **shah**-deh
That's life.	So geht's eben.	zoh gayts **ay**-ben
No problem.	Kein Problem.	kīn proh-**blaym**
O.K.	O.K.	"O.K."
This is the good life!	So ist das Leben schön!	zoh ist dahs **lay**-ben shurn
Good luck!	Viel Glück!	feel glewk
Let's go!	Auf geht's!	owf gayts

Thanks a million:

Thank you very much.	**Vielen Dank.**	fee-len dahngk
You are...	**Sie sind...**	zee zint
...helpful.	**...hilfreich.**	**hilf**-rīkh
...wonderful.	**...wunderbar.**	**voon**-der-bar
...generous.	**...großzügig.**	**grohs**-tsew-gig
This is great fun.	**Das macht viel Spaß.**	dahs mahkht feel shpahs
You've gone to much trouble.	**Sie haben sich soviel Mühe gemacht.**	zee **hah**-ben sikh zoh-feel **mew**-heh geh-**mahkht**
You are an angel from God.	**Sie sind ein Engel, von Gott gesandt.**	zee zint īn **eng**-el fon got geh-**zahndt**
You spoil me / us.	**Sie verwöhnen mich / uns.**	zee fehr-**vur**-nen mikh / oons
I will remember you...	**Ich werde Sie... in Erinnerung behalten.**	ikh **vehr**-deh zee... in ehr-**rin**-eh-roong beh-**hahl**-ten
...always.	**...immer**	**im**-mer
...till Tuesday.	**...bis Dienstag**	bis **deen**-stahg

Conversing with German animals:

rooster / cock-a-doodle-doo	**Hahn / kikeriki**	hahn / kee-keh-ree-**kee**
bird / tweet tweet	**Vogel / piep piep**	**foh**-gel / peep peep
cat / meow	**Katze / miau**	**kaht**-seh / mee-**ow**
dog / woof woof	**Hund / wuff wuff**	hoont / vuff vuff
duck / quack quack	**Ente / quak quak**	**en**-teh / kwahk kwahk
cow / moo	**Kuh / muh**	koo / moo
pig / oink oink	**Schwein / nöff nöff**	shvīn / nurf nurf

Create Your Own Conversation

You can mix and match these words into a
conversation. Make it as deep or silly as you want.

Who:

I / you	**ich / Sie**	ikh / zee
he / she	**er / sie**	er / zee
we / they	**wir / sie**	veer / zee
my / your...	**mein / ihre...**	mīn / eer
...parents / children	**...Eltern / Kinder**	**el**-tern / **kin**-der
men / women	**Männer / Frauen**	**men**-ner / **frow**-en
rich / poor	**Reichen / Armen**	**rīkh**-en / **ar**-men
politicians	**Politiker**	poh-**lit**-i-ker
big business	**Großkapital**	**grohs**-kahp-i-tahl
mafia	**Mafia**	**mah**-fee-ah
military	**Militär**	mil-ee-**tehr**
Neo-Nazis	**Neonazis**	"Neo-Nazis"
eastern Germany	**Ostdeutschland**	**ost**-doych-lahnd
western Germany	**Westen von Deutschland**	**ves**-ten fon **doych**-lahnd
Germans	**Deutschen**	**doy**-chen
Austrians	**Österreicher**	**urs**-teh-rīkh-er
Swiss	**Schweizer**	**shvīt**-ser
French	**Franzosen**	frahn-**tsoh**-zen
Italians	**Italiener**	i-tah-lee-**ehn**-er
Americans	**Amerikaner**	ah-mehr-ee-**kahn**-er
liberals	**Liberale**	**lib**-eh-rah-leh
conservatives	**Konservative**	**kohn**-zehr-vah-tiv-eh
radicals	**Radikale**	**rah**-di-kah-leh

travelers	**Reisende**	**rī**-zen-deh
everyone	**alle Leute**	**ah**-leh **loy**-teh
God	**Gott**	got

What:

want / need	**wollen / brauchen**	**vol**-len / **browkh**-en
take / give	**nehmen / geben**	**nay**-men / **gay**-ben
love / hate	**lieben / hassen**	**lee**-ben / **hah**-sen
work / play	**arbeiten / spielen**	**ar**-bīt-en / **shpeel**-en
have / lack	**haben / haben nicht**	**hah**-ben / **hah**-ben nikht
learn / fear	**lernen / fürchten**	**lern**-en / **fewrkh**-ten
help / abuse	**helfen / mißbrauchen**	**hel**-fen / mis-**broykh**-en
prosper / suffer	**florieren / leiden**	floh-**ree**-ren / **lī**-den
buy / sell	**kaufen / verkaufen**	**kow**-fen / **fehr**-kow-fen

Why:

love	**Liebe**	**lee**-beh
sex	**Sex**	sex
money	**Geld**	gelt
power	**Macht**	mahkht
work	**Arbeit**	**ar**-bīt
food	**Essen**	**es**-sen
family	**Familie**	fah-**mee**-lee-eh
health	**Gesundheit**	geh-**zoond**-hīt
hope	**Hoffnung**	**hof**-noong
education	**Ausbildung**	**ows**-bil-doong
guns	**Waffen**	**vah**-fen

religion	**Religion**	reh-leeg-ee-**ohn**
happiness	**Glück**	glewk
marijuana	**Marihuana**	**mah**-ri-wah-nah
democracy	**Demokratie**	day-moh-krah-**tee**
taxes	**Steuern**	**shtoy**-ern
lies	**Lügen**	**lew**-gen
corruption	**Korruption**	kor-rupt-see-**ohn**
pollution	**Umweltver-schmutzung**	**oom**-velt-fehr-**shmut**-tsoong
television	**Fernsehen**	fern-**zay**-hen
relaxation	**Entspannung**	ent-**shpah**-noong
violence	**Gewalt**	geh-**vahlt**
reunification	**Wiedervereinigung**	**vee**-dehr-fehr-īn-i-goong
respect	**Respekt**	res-**pekt**
racism	**Rassimus**	rah-**sis**-moos
war / peace	**Krieg / Frieden**	kreeg / **free**-den
global perspective	**Gesamtperspektive**	geh-**zahmt**-per-spek-ti-veh

You be the judge:

(no) problem	**(kein) Problem**	(kīn) proh-**blaym**
(not) good	**(nicht) gut**	(nikht) goot
(not) dangerous	**(nicht) gefährlich**	(nikht) geh-**fayr**-likh
(not) fair	**(nicht) fair**	(nikht) "fair"
(not) guilty	**(nicht) schuldig**	(nikht) **shool**-dig
(not) powerful	**(nicht) mächtig**	(nikht) **mekh**-tig
(not) stupid	**(nicht) dumm**	(nikht) dum
(not) happy	**(nicht) glücklich**	(nikht) **glewk**-likh
because / for	**weil / wegen**	vīl / **vay**-gen

CHATTING

and / or / from	**und / oder / von**	oont / **oh**-der / fon
too much	**zu viel**	tsoo feel
enough	**genug**	geh-**noog**
never enough	**nie genug**	nee geh-**noog**
worse	**schlechter**	**shlekh**-ter
same	**gleich**	glīkh
better	**besser**	**bes**-ser
here	**hier**	heer
everywhere	**überall**	ew-ber-**ahl**

Assorted beginnings and endings:

I like...	**Ich mag...**	ikh mahg
I don't like...	**Ich mag... nicht.**	ikh mahg... nikht
Do you like...?	**Mögen Sie...?**	**mur**-gen zee
In the past...	**Früher...**	**frew**-her
I am / Are you...?	**Ich bin / Sind Sie...?**	ikh bin / zint zee
...an optimist / pessimist	**...ein Optimist / Pessimist**	īn opt-i-**meest** / pes-i-**meest**
I believe in...	**Ich glaube an...**	ikh **glow**-beh ahn
I don't believe in...	**Ich glaube nicht an...**	ikh **glow**-beh nikht ahn
Do you believe in...?	**Glauben Sie an...?**	**glow**-ben zee ahn
...God	**...Gott**	got
...life after death	**...Leben nach dem Tod**	**lay**-ben nahkh daym tod
...extraterrestrial life	**...Leben im Weltall**	**lay**-ben im **velt**-ahl
...Santa Claus	**...Weihnachtsmann**	vī-**nahkhts**-mahn
Yes. / No.	**Ja. / Nein.**	yah / nīn
Maybe.	**Vielleicht.**	fee-**līkht**

I don't know.	**Ich weiß nicht.**	ikh vīs nikht
What is most important in life?	**Was ist das Wichtigste im Leben?**	vahs ist dahs **vikh**-tig-steh im **lay**-ben
The problem is...	**Das Problem ist...**	dahs proh-**blaym** ist
The answer is...	**Die Antwort ist...**	dee **ahnt**-vort ist
We have solved the world's problems.	**Wir haben die Probleme der Welt gelöst.**	veer **hah**-ben dee proh-**blay**-meh dehr velt geh-**lurst**

A German Romance

Words of love:

I / me / you	**ich / mich / dich**	ikh / mikh / dikh
flirt	**flirten**	**flir**-ten
kiss	**Kuß**	kus
hug	**Umarmung**	oom-**ar**-mung
love	**Liebe**	**lee**-beh
make love (sleep together)	**miteinander schlafen**	mit-īn-**ahn**-dehr **shlah**-fen
condom	**Präservativ, Kondom**	pray-zehr-fah-**tif**, **kon**-dohm
contraceptive	**Verhütungsmittel**	fehr-**hew**-toongs-**mit**-tel
safe sex	**safe sex**	"safe sex"
sexy	**sexy**	"sexy"
cozy	**gemütlich**	geh-**mewt**-likh
romantic	**romantisch**	roh-**mahn**-tish
cupcake	**Schnuckel**	**shnuk**-el
little rabbit	**Häschen**	**hays**-khen

| little sugar mouse | **Zuckermäuschen** | **tsoo**-ker-**moys**-khen |
| pussy cat | **Miezekatze** | **meets**-eh-**kaht**-seh |

Ah, Liebe:

What's the matter?	**Was ist los?**	vahs ist lohs
Nothing.	**Nichts.**	nikhts
I am / Are you...?	**Ich bin / Sind Sie...?**	ikh bin / zint zee
...straight	**...hetero**	**hay**-ter-oh
...gay	**...schwul**	shvul
...undecided	**...mir nicht sicher**	meer nikht **zikh**-er
...prudish	**...verklemmt**	fehr-**klemt**
...horny	**...geil**	gīl
We are on our honeymoon.	**Wir sind auf unserer Hochzeitsreise.**	veer zint owf **oon**-zer-er **hokh**-tsīts-rī-zeh
I have...	**Ich habe...**	ikh **hah**-beh
...a boyfriend.	**...einen Freund.**	**ī**-nen froynd
...a girlfriend.	**...eine Freundin.**	**ī**-neh **froyn**-din
I am (not) married.	**Ich bin (nicht) verheiratet.**	ikh bin (nikht) fehr-**hī**-rah-tet
I am rich and single.	**Ich bin reich und zu haben.**	ikh bin rīkh oont tsoo **hah**-ben
I am lonely.	**Ich bin einsam.**	ikh bin **īn**-zahm
I have no diseases.	**Ich habe keine Krankheiten.**	ikh **hah**-beh **kī**-neh **krahnk**-hī-ten
I have many diseases.	**Ich habe viele Krankheiten.**	ikh **hah**-beh **fee**-leh **krahnk**-hī-ten
Can I see you again?	**Können wir uns wiedersehen?**	**kurn**-nen veer oons **vee**-der-zayn

You are my most beautiful souvenir.	Du bist mein schönstes Andenken.	doo bist mīn shurn-stes ahn-denk-en
Is this an aphrodisiac?	Ist dies ein Aphrodisiakum?	ist deez īn ah-froh-dee-zee-ahk-oom
This is (not) my first time.	Dies ist für mich (nicht) das erste Mal.	deez ist fewr mikh (nikht) dahs ehr-steh mahl
Do you do this often?	Machst du das oft?	mahkhst doo dahs oft
How's my breath?	Habe ich Mundgeruch?	hah-beh ikh mund-geh-rukh
Let's just be friends.	Wir können doch einfach Freunde sein.	veer kurn-nen dokh īn-fahkh froyn-deh zīn
I'll pay for my share.	Ich bezahle meinen Anteil.	ikh beht-sah-leh mī-nen ahn-tīl
Would you like a... massage?	Darf ich dir den... massieren?	darf ikh deer dayn... mah-see-ren
...foot	...Fuß	foos
...back	...Rücken	rew-ken
Why not?	Warum nicht?	vah-room nikht
Try it.	Versuch's doch mal.	fehr-zookhs dokh mahl
That tickles.	Das kitzelt.	dahs kit-selt
Oh my God!	Oh mein Gott!	oh mīn got
I love you.	Ich liebe dich.	ikh lee-beh dikh
Darling, marry me!	Liebling, heirate mich!	lee-bleeng hī-rah-teh mikh

English - German Dictionary

A

above über
accident Unfall
accountant Buchhalter
adaptor Zwischenstecker
address Adresse
adult Erwachsener
afraid ängstlich
after nach
afternoon Nachmittag
aftershave Rasierwasser
afterwards nachher
again noch einmal
age Alter
aggressive aggressiv
agree einverstanden
AIDS AIDS
air Luft
air-conditioned Klimaanlage
air mail Luftpost
airline Fluggesellschaft
airport Flughafen
alarm clock Wecker
alcohol Alkohol
allergic allergisch
allergies Allergien
alone allein
already schon
always immer
ancestor Vorfahre
ancient altertümlich
and und
angry wütend

ankle Fußknöchel
animal Tier
another noch ein
answer Antwort
antibiotic Antibiotika
antiques Antiquitäten
apartment Wohnung
apology Entschuldigung
appetizers Vorspeise
apple Apfel
appointment Verabredung
approximately ungefähr
arm Arm
arrivals Ankunften
arrive ankommen
art Kunst
artificial künstlich
artist Künstler
ashtray Aschenbecher
ask fragen
aspirin Aspirin
at bei
attractive attraktiv
aunt Tante
Austria Österreich
autumn Herbst

B

baby Baby
babysitter Babysitter
backpack Rucksack
bad schlecht
bag Tüte

baggage Gepäck
bakery Bäckerei
balcony Balkon
ball Ball
banana Banane
band-aid Pflaster
bank Bank
barber Frisör
basement Keller
basket Korb
bath Bad
bathroom Bad
bathtub Badewanne
battery Batterie
beach Strand
beard Bart
beautiful schön
because weil
bed Bett
bedroom Zimmer
bedsheet Laken
beef Rindfleisch
beer Bier
before vor
begin anfangen
behind hinter
below unter
belt Gürtel
best am besten
better besser
bib Lätzchen
bicycle Fahrrad
big groß
bill (payment) Rechnung
bird Vogel
birthday Geburtstag

black schwarz
blanket Decke
blond blond
blood Blut
blouse Bluse
blue blau
boat Schiff
body Körper
boiled gekocht
bomb Bombe
book Buch
book shop Buchladen
boots Stiefel
border Grenze
borrow leihen
boss Boss
bottle Flasche
bottom Boden
bowl Schale
box Karton
boy Junge
bra B.H.
bracelet Armband
bread Brot
breakfast Frühstück
bridge Brücke
briefs Unterhosen
Britain England
broken kaputt
brother Bruder
brown braun
bucket Eimer
building Gebäude
bulb Birne
burn (n) Verbrennung
bus Bus

business Geschäft
business card visitenkarte
but aber
button Knopf
buy kaufen
by (via) mit

C

calendar Kalender
calorie Kalorie
camera Photoapparat
camping Camping
can (n) Dose
can (v) können
can opener Dosenöffner
Canada Kanada
canal Kanal
candle Kerze
candy Bonbons
canoe Kanu
cap Deckel
captain Kapitän
car Auto
carafe Karaffe
card Karte
cards (deck) Karten
careful vorsichtig
carpet Teppich
carry tragen
cashier Kassierer
cassette Kassette
castle Burg
cat Katze
catch (v) fangen
cathedral Kathedrale

cave Höhle
cellar Keller
center Zentrum
century Jahrhundert
chair Stuhl
change (n) Wechsel
change (v) wechseln
charming bezaubernd
cheap billig
check Scheck
Cheers! Prost!
cheese Käse
chicken Hühnchen
children Kinder
Chinese (adj) chinesisches
chocolate Schokolade
Christmas Weihnachten
church Kirche
cigarette Zigarette
cinema Kino
city Stadt
class Klasse
clean (adj) sauber
clear klar
cliff Kliff
closed geschlossen
cloth Stoff
clothes Kleider
clothes pins Wäscheklammern
clothesline Wäscheleine
cloudy bewölkt
coast Küste
coat Jacke
coat hanger Kleiderbügel
coffee Kaffee
coins Münzen

cold (adj) kalt
colors Farben
comb (n) Kamm
come kommen
comfortable komfortabel
compact disc C.D.
complain sich beschweren
complicated kompliziert
computer Komputer
concert Konzert
condom Präservativ
conductor Schaffner
confirm konfirmieren
congratulations Glückwünsche
connection (train) Anschluß
constipation Verstopfung
cook (v) kochen
cool kühl
cork Korken
corkscrew Korkenzieher
corner Ecke
corridor Flur
cost (v) kosten
cot Liege
cotton Baumwolle
cough (v) husten
cough drops Hustenpastillen
country Land
countryside auf dem Land
cousin Vetter
cow Kuh
cozy gemütlich
crafts Kunstgewerbe
cream Sahne
credit card Kreditkarte
crib Kinderbett
crowd (n) Menge

cry (v) weinen
cup Tasse

D

dad Papa
dance (v) tanzen
danger Gefahr
dangerous gefährlich
dark dunkel
daughter Tochter
day Tag
dead tot
delay Verspätung
delicious lecker
dental floss Zahnseide
dentist Zahnarzt
deodorant Deodorant
depart abfahren
departures Abfahrten
deposit Kaution
dessert Nachtisch
detour Umleitung
diabetic diabetisch
diamond Diamant
diaper Windel
diarrhea Durchfall
dictionary Wörterbuch
die sterben
difficult schwierig
dinner Abendessen
direct direkt
direction Richtung
dirty schmutzig
discount Ermäßigung
disease Krankheit

disturb stören
divorced geschieden
doctor Arzt
dog Hund
doll Puppe
donkey Esel
door Tür
dormitory Schlafsaal
double doppel
down runter
dream (n) Traum
dream (v) träumen
dress (n) Kleid
drink (n) Getränk
drive (v) fahren
driver Fahrer
drunk betrunken
dry trocken

E

each jede
ear Ohr
early früh
earplugs Ohrenschützer
earrings Ohrringe
earth Erde
east Osten
Easter Ostern
easy einfach
eat essen
elbow Ellbogen
elevator Fahrstuhl
embarrassing peinlich
embassy Botschaft
empty leer

engineer Ingenieur
English Englisch
enjoy genießen
enough genug
entrance Eingang
entry Eingang
envelope Briefumschlag
eraser Radiergummi
especially besonders
Europe Europa
evening Abend
every jede
everything alles
exactly genau
example Beispiel
excellent ausgezeichnet
except außer
exchange (n) Wechsel
excuse me Entschuldigung
exhausted erschöpft
exit Ausgang
expensive teuer
explain erklären
eye Auge

F

face Gesicht
factory Fabrik
fall (v) fallen
false falsch
family Familie
famous berühmt
fantastic phantastisch
far weit
farm Bauernhof

farmer Bauer
fashion Mode
fat (adj) fett
father Vater
father-in-law Schwiegervater
faucet Wasserhahn
female weiblich
ferry Fähre
festival Festival
fever Fieber
few wenig
field Feld
fight (n) Streit
fight (v) streiten
fine (good) gut
finger Finger
finish (v) beenden
fireworks Feuerwerk
first erst
first aid Erste Hilfe
first class erste Klasse
fish Fisch
fish (v) fischen
fix (v) reparieren
fizzy sprudelnd
flag Fahne
flashlight Taschenlampe
flavor (n) Geschmack
flea Floh
flight Flug
flower Blume
flu Grippe
fly fliegen
fog Nebel
food Essen
foot Fuß
football Fußball

for für
forbidden verboten
foreign fremd
forget vergessen
fork Gabel
fountain Brunnen
France Frankreich
free (no cost) umsonst
fresh frisch
Friday Freitag
friend Freund
friendship Freundschaft
frisbee Frisbee
from von
fruit Obst
fun Spaß
funeral Beerdigung
funny komisch
furniture Möbel
future Zukunft

G

gallery Galerie
game Spiel
garage Garage
garden Garten
gardening Gärtnern
gas Benzin
gas station Tankstelle
gay schwul
gentleman Herr
genuine echt
Germany Deutschland
gift Geschenk
girl Mädchen

give geben
glass Glas
glasses (eye) Brille
gloves Handschuhe
go gehen
go through durchgehen
God Gott
gold Gold
golf Golf
good gut
good day guten Tag
goodbye auf Wiedersehen
grammar Grammatik
granddaughter Enkelin
grandfather Großvater
grandmother Großmutter
grandson Enkel
gray grau
greasy fettig
great super
Greece Griechenland
green grün
grocery store Lebensmittelgeschäft
guarantee Garantie
guest Gast
guide Führer
guidebook Führer
guitar Gitarre
gum Kaugummi
gun Gewehr

H

hair Haare
hairbrush Haarbürste
haircut Frisur
hand Hand
handicapped behindert
handicrafts Handarbeiten
handiwipes Wischtücher
handle (n) Griff
handsome gutaussehend
happy glücklich
harbor Hafen
hard hart
hat Hut
hate (v) hassen
have haben
he er
head Kopf
headache Kopfschmerzen
healthy gesund
hear hören
heart Herz
heat (v) aufwarmen
heat (n) Hitze
heaven Himmel
heavy schwer
hello hallo
helmet Helm
help (n) Hilfe
hemorrhoids Hämorrholden
her ihr
here hier
hi hallo
high hoch
highchair Kinderstuhl
highway Landstraße
hike wandern
hill Hügel
history Geschichte
hitchhike per Anhalter fahren

hobby Hobby
hole Loch
holiday Feiertag
homemade hausgemacht
homesick Heimweh
honest ehrlich
honeymoon Hochzeitsreise
horrible schrecklich
horse Pferd
horse riding reiten
hospital Krankenhaus
hot heiß
hotel Hotel
hour Stunde
house Haus
how wie
how many wieviele
how much ($) wieviel kostet
hungry hungrig
hurry (v) sich beeilen
husband Ehemann
hydrofoil Tragflächenboot

incredible unglaublich
independent unabhängig
indigestion Verdauungs-
störung
industry Industrie
infection Entzündung
information Information
injured verletzt
innocent unschuldig
insect Insekt
insect repellant Mückenspray
inside innen
instant sofortig
instead anstatt
insurance Versicherung
intelligent klug
interesting interessant
invitation Einladung
iodine Jod
is ist
island Insel
Italy Italien

I

I ich
ice Eis
ice cream Eis
if ob
ill krank
immediately sofort
important wichtig
imported importiert
impossible unmöglich
in in
included eingeschlossen

J

jacket Jacke
jaw Kiefer
jeans Jeans
jewelry Schmuck
job Beruf
jogging Jogging
joke (n) Witz
journey Reise
juice Saft
jump (v) springen

K

keep behalten
kettle Kessel
key Schlüssel
kill töten
kind freundlich
king König
kiss Küß
kitchen Küche
knee Knie
knife Messer
know wissen

L

ladder Leiter
ladies Damen
lake See
lamb Lamm
lamp Lampe
language Sprache
large groß
last letzte
late spät
later später
laugh (v) lachen
laundromat Waschsalon
lawyer Anwalt
lazy faul
leather Leder
leave gehen
left links
leg Bein
lend leihen
letter Brief

library Leihbücherei
life Leben
light (n) Licht
light bulb Glühbirne
lighter (n) Feuerzeug
like (v) mögen
lip Lippe
list Liste
listen zuhören
liter Liter
little (adj) klein
live leben
local örtlich
lock (v) abschließen
lock (n) Schloß
lockers Schließfächer
look gucken
lost verloren
loud laut
love (v) lieben
lover Liebhaber
low niedrig
lozenges Halsbonbon
luck Glück
luggage Gepäck
lukewarm lau
lungs Lungen

M

macho macho
mad wütend
magazine Zeitschrift
mail (n) Post
main Haupt
make (v) machen

male männlich
man Mann
manager Geschäftsführer
many viele
map Karte
market Markt
married verheiratet
matches Streichhölzer
maximum Maximum
maybe vielleicht
meat Fleisch
medicine Medikamente
medium mittel
men Herren
menu Speisekarte
message Nachricht
metal Metall
midnight Mitternacht
mineral water Mineralwasser
minimum Minimum
minutes Minuten
mirror Spiegel
Miss Fräulein
mistake Fehler
misunderstanding
  Mißverständnis
mix (n) Mischung
modern modern
moment Moment
Monday Montag
money Geld
month Monat
monument Denkmal
moon Mond
more mehr
morning Morgen
mosquito Mücke

mother Mutter
mother-in-law Schwiegermutter
mountain Berg
moustache Schnurrbart
mouth Mund
movie Film
Mr. Herr
Mrs. Frau
much viel
muscle Muskel
museum Museum
music Musik
my mein

N

nail clipper Nagelschere
naked nackt
name Name
napkin Serviette
narrow schmal
nationality Nationalität
natural natürlich
nature Natur
nausea Übelkeit
near nahe
necessary notwendig
necklace Kette
need brauchen
needle Nadel
nephew Neffe
nervous nervös
never nie
new neu
newspaper Zeitung
next nächste

nice nett
nickname Spitzname
niece Nichte
night Nacht
no nein
no vacancy belegt
noisy laut
non-smoking Nichtraucher
noon Mittag
normal normal
north Norden
nose Nase
not nicht
notebook Notizbuch
nothing nichts
now jetzt

O

occupation Beruf
occupied besetzt
ocean Meer
of von
office Büro
O.K. O.K.
old alt
on auf
once einmal
one way (street) einfach
one way (ticket) Hinfahrkarte
only nur
open (adj) offen
open (v) öffnen
opera Oper
operator Vermittlung
optician Optiker

or oder
orange (color) orange
orange (fruit) Apfelsine
original Original
other anderes
outdoors im Freien
oven Ofen
over (finished) beendet
own (v) besitzen
owner Besitzer

P

pacifier Schnuller
package Paket
page Seite
pail Eimer
pain Schmerz
painting Gemälde
palace Schloß
panties Unterhosen
pants Hosen
paper Papier
paper clip Büroklammer
parents Eltern
park (v) parken
park (garden) Park
party Party
passenger Reisende
passport Paß
pay bezahlen
peace Frieden
pedestrian Fußgänger
pen Kugelschreiber
pencil Bleistift
people Leute

percent Prozent
perfect perfekt
perfume Parfum
period (of time) Zeitabschnitt
period (woman's) Periode
person Person
pet (n) Haustier
pharmacy Apotheke
photo Photo
photocopy Fotokopie
pick-pocket Taschendieb
picnic Picknick
piece Stück
pig Schwein
pill Pille
pillow Kissen
pin Nadel
pink rosa
pity, it's a wie schade
pizza Pizza
plain einfach
plane Flugzeug
plant Pflanze
plastic Plastik
plastic bag Plastiktüte
plate Teller
platform (train) Bahnsteig
play (v) spielen
play Theater
please bitte
pliers Zange
pocket Tasche
point (v) zeigen
police Polizei
poor arm
pork Schweinefleisch
possible möglich

postcard Postkarte
poster Poster
practical praktisch
pregnant schwanger
prescription Rezept
present (gift) Geschenk
pretty hübsch
price Preis
priest Priester
private privat
problem Problem
profession Beruf
prohibited verboten
pronunciation Aussprache
public öffentlich
pull ziehen
purple violett
purse Handtasche
push drücken

Q

quality Qualität
quarter (¼) Viertel
queen Königin
question (n) Frage
quiet ruhig

R

R.V. Wohnwagen
rabbit Hase
radio Radio
raft Floß
railway Eisenbahn
rain (n) Regen

rainbow Regenbogen
raincoat Regenmantel
rape (n) Vergewaltigung
raw roh
razor Rasierer
ready bereit
receipt Beleg
receive erhalten
receptionist Empfangsperson
recipe Rezept
recommend empfehlen
red rot
refill (v) nachschenken
refund (n) Rückgabe
relax (v) sich erholen
religion Religion
remember sich erinnern
rent (v) mieten
repair (v) reparieren
repeat noch einmal
reservation Reservierung
reserve reservieren
return zurückgeben
rich reich
right rechts
ring (n) Ring
ripe reif
river Fluß
rock (n) Fels
roller skates Rollschuhe
romantic romantisch
roof Dach
room Zimmer
rope Seil
rotten verdorben
roundtrip Rückfahrt
rowboat Ruderboot

rucksack Rucksack
rug Teppich
ruins Ruine
run (v) laufen

S

sad traurig
safe sicher
safety pin Sicherheitsnadel
sailing segeln
sale Ausverkauf
same gleiche
sandals Sandalen
sandwich belegtes Brot
sanitary napkins Damenbinden
Saturday Samstag
scandalous sündig
scarf Schal
school Schule
science Wissenschaft
scientist Wissenschaftler
scissors Schere
scotch tape Tesafilm
screwdriver Schraubenzieher
sculptor Bildhauer
sculpture Skulptur
sea Meer
seafood Meeresfrüchte
seat Platz
second zweite
second class zweiter Klasse
secret Geheimnis
see sehen
self-service Selbstbedienung

sell verkaufen	**sister** Schwester
send senden	**size** Größe
separate (adj) getrennt	**skating (ice)** Eislaufen
serious ernsthaft	**ski (v)** skilaufen
service Bedienung	**skin** Haut
sex Sex	**skinny** dünn
sexy sexy	**skirt** Rock
shampoo Shampoo	**sky** Himmel
shaving cream Rasiercreme	**sleep (v)** schlafen
she sie	**sleepy** schläfrig
sheet Laken	**slice** Scheibe
shell Schale	**slide (photo)** Dia
ship (v) schicken	**slippery** glatt
ship (n) Schiff	**slow** langsam
shirt Hemd	**small** klein
shoes Schuhe	**smell (n)** Geruch
shopping einkaufen	**smile (n)** Lächeln
short kurz	**smoking** Rauchen
shorts shorts	**snack** Imbiß
shoulder Schulter	**sneeze (n)** Niesen
show (n) Vorführung	**snore** schnarchen
show (v) zeigen	**snow** Schnee
shower Dusche	**soap** Seife
shy ängstlich	**soccer** Fußball
sick krank	**socks** Socken
sign Schild	**something** etwas
signature Unterschrift	**son** Sohn
silence Ruhe	**song** Lied
silk Seide	**soon** bald
silver Silber	**sorry** Entschuldigung
similar ähnlich	**sour** sauer
simple einfach	**south** Süden
sing singen	**speak** sprechen
singer Sänger	**specialty** Spezialität
single ledig	**speed** Geschwindigkeit
sink Waschbecken	**spend** ausgeben
sir mein Herr	**spider** Spinne

spoon Löffel
sport Sport
spring Frühling
square (town) Platz
stairs Treppe
stamp Briefmarke
stapler Klammeraffe
star (in sky) Stern
state Staat
station Station
stomach Magen
stop (n) Halt
stop (v) halten
storm Sturm
story (floor) Stock
straight geradeaus
strange merkwürdig
stream (n) Fluß
street Straße
strike (no work) Streik
string Leine
strong stark
stuck festsitzen
student Student
stupid dumm
sturdy haltbar
style Stil
suddenly plötzlich
suitcase Koffer
summer Sommer
sun Sonne
sunbathe sich sonnen
sunburn Sonnenbrand
Sunday Sonntag
sunglasses Sonnenbrille
sunny sonnig
sunset Sonnenuntergang

sunscreen Sonnencreme
sunshine Sonnenschein
sunstroke Sonnenstich
suntan (n) Sonnenbräune
suntan lotion Sonnenöl
supermarket Supermarkt
supplement Zuschlag
surprise (n) Überraschung
swallow (v) schlucken
sweat (v) schwitzen
sweater Pullover
sweet süß
swim schwimmen
swim trunks Badehose
swimming pool Schwimmbad
swimsuit Badeanzug
Switzerland Schweiz
synthetic synthetisch

T

table Tisch
tall Schwanz
take nehmen
take out (food) mitnehmen
talcum powder Babypuder
talk reden
tall hoch
tampons Tampons
tape (cassette) Kassette
taste (n) Gaschmack
taste (v) probieren
tax Steuer
teacher Lehrer
team Team
teenager Jugendlicher

telephone Telefon
television Fernsehen
temperature Temperatur
tender zart
tennis Tennis
tennis shoes Turnschuhe
tent Zelt
tent pegs Zelthäringe
terrible schrecklich
thanks danke
theater Theater
thermometer Thermometer
they sie
thick dick
thief Dieb
thigh Schenkel
thin dünn
thing Ding
think denken
thirsty durstig
thongs Badelatschen
thread Faden
throat Hals
through durch
throw werfen
Thursday Donnerstag
ticket Eintrittskarte
tight eng
timetable Fahrplan
tired müde
tissues Taschentuch
to nach
today heute
toe Zeh
together zusammen
toilet Toilette

toilet paper Klopapier
tomorrow morgen
tonight heute abend
too zu
tooth Zahn
toothbrush Zahnbürste
toothpaste Zahnpasta
toothpick Zahnstocher
total Völlig
tour Tour
tourist Tourist
towel Handtuch
tower Turm
town Stadt
toy Spielzeug
track (train) Gleis
traditional traditionell
traffic Verkehr
train Zug
translate übersetzen
travel reisen
travel agency Reisebüro
traveler's check Reisescheck
tree Baum
trip Fahrt
trouble Schwierigkeiten
T-shirt T-Shirt
Tuesday Dienstag
tunnel Tunnel
tweezers Pinzette
twins Zwillinge

U

ugly häßlich
umbrella Regenschirm

uncle Onkel
under unter
underpants Unterhose
understand verstehen
underwear Unterwäsche
unemployed arbeitslos
unfortunately unglücklicher-
  weise
United States Vereinigte Staaten
university Universität
up hoch
upstairs oben
urgent dringend
us uns
use nutzen

V

vacancy (sign) Zimmer frei
vacant frei
valley Tal
vegetarian (n) Vegetarier
very sehr
vest Jacke
video Video
video camera Videokamera
video recorder Videogerät
view Blick
village Dorf
vineyard Weinberg
virus Virus
visit (n) Besuch
visit (v) besuchen
vitamins Vitamine
voice Stimme
vomit (v) sich übergeben

W

waist Taille
wait warten
waiter Kellner
waitress Kellnerin
wake up aufwachen
walk (v) gehen
wallet Brieftasche
want möchte
warm (adj) warm
wash waschen
watch (v) beobachten
watch (n) Uhr
water Wasser
water, tap Leitungswasser
waterfall Wasserfall
we wir
weather Wetter
weather forecast
  Wettervorhersage
wedding Hochzeit
Wednesday Mittwoch
week Woche
weight Gewicht
welcome willkommen
west Westen
wet naß
what was
wheel Rad
when wann
where wo
whipped cream Schlagsahne
white weiß
white-out Tipp-Ex
who wer

why warum
widow Witwe
widower Witwer
wife Ehefrau
wild wild
wind Wind
window Fenster
wine Wein
wing Flügel
winter Winter
wish (v) wünschen
with mit
without ohne
women Damen
wood Holz
wool Wolle
word Wort
work (n) Arbeit
work (v) arbeiten
world Welt
worse schlechter
worst schlechteste
wrap umwickeln
write schreiben

Y

year Jahr
yellow gelb
yes ja
yesterday gestern
you (formal) Sie
you (informal) du
young jung
youth hostel Jugendherberge

Z

zero null
zip-lock bag Gefrierbeutel
zipper Reißverschluß
zoo Zoo

DICTIONARY

German-English Dictionary

A

Abend evening
Abendessen dinner
aber but
abfahren depart
Abfahrten departures
abschließen lock (v)
Adresse address
aggressiv aggressive
ähnlich similar
AIDS AIDS
Alkohol alcohol
allein alone
Allergien allergies
allergisch allergic
alles everything
alt old
Alter age
altertümlich ancient
am besten best
anderes other
anfangen begin
ängstlich afraid
ängstlich shy
ankommen arrive
Ankunften arrivals
Anschluß connection (train)
anstatt instead
Antibiotika antibiotic
Antiquitäten antiques
Antwort answer
Anwalt lawyer
Apfel apple

Apfelsine orange (fruit)
Apotheke pharmacy
Arbeit work (n)
arbeiten work (v)
arbeitslos unemployed
Arm arm
arm poor
Armband bracelet
Arzt doctor
Aschenbecher ashtray
Aspirin aspirin
attraktiv attractive
auf on
auf dem Land countryside
auf Wiedersehen goodbye
aufwachen wake up
Auge eye
aurwarmen heat (v)
außer except
Ausgang exit
ausgeben spend
ausgezeichnet excellent
Aussprache pronunciation
Ausverkauf sale
Auto car

B

B.H. bra
Baby baby
Babypuder talcum powder
Babysitter babysitter
Bäckerei bakery
Bad bath

Bad bathroom
Badeanzug swim suit
Badehose swim trunks
Badelatschen thongs
Badewanne bathtub
Bahnsteig platform (train)
bald soon
Balkon balcony
Ball ball
Banane banana
Bank bank
Bart beard
Batterie battery
Bauer farmer
Bauernhof farm
Baum tree
Baumwolle cotton
Bedienung service
beenden finish (v)
beendet over (finished)
Beerdigung funeral
behalten keep
behindert handicapped
bei at
Bein leg
Beispiel example
Beleg receipt
belegt no vacancy
belegtes Brot sandwich
Benzin gas
beobachten watch (v)
bereit ready
Berg mountain
Beruf job
Beruf occupation
Beruf profession
berühmt famous

besetzt occupied
besitzen own (v)
Besitzer owner
besonders especially
besser better
Besuch visit (n)
besuchen visit (v)
betrunken drunk
Bett bed
bewölkt cloudy
bezahlen pay
bezaubernd charming
Bier beer
Bildhauer sculptor
billig cheap
Birne bulb
bitte please
blau blue
Bleistift pencil
Blick view
blond blond
Blume flower
Bluse blouse
Blut blood
Boden bottom
Bombe bomb
Bonbons candy
Boss boss
Botschaft embassy
brauchen need
braun brown
Brief letter
Briefmarke stamp
Brieftasche wallet
Briefumschlag envelope
Brille glasses (eye)
Brot bread

Brücke bridge
Bruder brother
Brunnen fountain
Buch book
Buchhalter accountant
Buchladen book shop
Burg castle
Büro office
Büroklammer paper clip
Bus bus

C

C.D. compact disc
Camping camping
chinesisches Chinese (adj)

D

Dach roof
Damen ladies
Damen women
Damenbinden sanitary napkins
danke thanks
Decke blanket
Deckel cap
denken think
Denkmal monument
Deodorant deodorant
Deutschland Germany
Dia slide (photo)
diabetisch diabetic
Diamant diamond
dick thick
Dieb thief

Dienstag Tuesday
Ding thing
direkt direct
Donnerstag Thursday
doppel double
Dorf village
Dose can (n)
Dosenöffner can opener
dringend urgent
drücken push
du you (informal)
dumm stupid
dunkel dark
dünn skinny
dünn thin
durch through
Durchfall diarrhea
durchgehen go through
durstig thirsty
Dusche shower

E

echt genuine
Ecke corner
Ehefrau wife
Ehemann husband
ehrlich honest
Eimer bucket
Eimer pail
einfach easy
einfach one way (street)
einfach plain
einfach simple
Eingang entrance
Eingang entry

eingeschlossen included
einkaufen shopping
Einladung invitation
einmal once
Eintrittskarte ticket
einverstanden agree
Eis ice
Eis ice cream
Eisenbahn railway
Eislaufen skating (ice)
Ellbogen elbow
Eltern parents
Empfangsperson receptionist
empfehlen recommend
eng tight
England Britain
Englisch English
Enkel grandson
Enkelin granddaughter
Entschuldigung apology
Entschuldigung excuse me
Entschuldigung sorry
Entzündung infection
er he
Erde earth
erhalten receive
erklären explain
Ermäßigung discount
ernsthaft serious
erschöpft exhausted
erst first
Erste Hilfe first aid
erste Klasse first class
Erwachsener adult
Esel donkey
essen eat
Essen food

etwas something
Europa Europe

F

Fabrik factory
Faden thread
Fahne flag
Fähre ferry
fahren drive (v)
Fahrer driver
Fahrplan timetable
Fahrrad bicycle
Fahrstuhl elevator
Fahrt trip
fallen fall (v)
falsch false
Familie family
fangen catch (v)
Farben colors
faul lazy
Fehler mistake
Feiertag holiday
Feld field
Fels rock (n)
Fenster window
Fernsehen television
Festival festival
festsitzen stuck
fett fat (adj)
fettig greasy
Feuerwerk fireworks
Feuerzeug lighter (n)
Fieber fever
Film movie
Finger finger

Fisch fish
fischen fish (v)
Flasche bottle
Fleisch meat
fliegen fly
Floh flea
Floß raft
Flug flight
Flügel wing
Fluggesellschaft airline
Flughafen airport
Flugzeug plane
Flur corridor
Fluß river
Fluß stream (n)
Fotokopie photocopy
Frage question (n)
fragen ask
Frankreich France
Frau Mrs.
Fräulein Miss
frei vacant
Freitag Friday
fremd foreign
Freund friend
freundlich kind
Freundschaft friendship
Frieden peace
Frisbee frisbee
frisch fresh
Frisör barber
Frisur haircut
früh early
Frühling spring
Frühstück breakfast
Führer guide
Führer guidebook

für for
Fuß foot
Fußball football
Fußball soccer
Fußgänger pedestrian
Fußknöchel ankle

G

Gabel fork
Galerie gallery
Garage garage
Garantie guarantee
Garten garden
Gärtnern gardening
Gaschmack taste (n)
Gast guest
Gebäude building
geben give
Geburtstag birthday
Gefahr danger
gefährlich dangerous
Gefrierbeutel zip-lock bag
Geheimnis secret
gehen go
gehen leave
gehen walk (v)
gekocht boiled
gelb yellow
Geld money
Gemälde painting
gemütlich cozy
genau exactly
genießen enjoy
genug enough
Gepäck baggage

Gepäck luggage
geradeaus straight
Geruch smell (n)
Geschäft business
Geschäftsführer manager
Geschenk gift
Geschenk present (gift)
Geschichte history
geschieden divorced
geschlossen closed
Geschmack flavor (n)
Geschwindigkeit speed
Gesicht face
gestern yesterday
gesund healthy
Getränk drink (n)
getrennt separate (adj)
Gewehr gun
Gewicht weight
Gitarre guitar
Glas glass
glatt slippery
gleiche same
Gleis track (train)
Glück luck
glücklich happy
Glückwünsche congratulations
Glühbirne light bulb
Gold gold
Golf golf
Gott God
Grammatik grammar
grau gray
Grenze border
Griechenland Greece
Griff handle (n)
Grippe flu

groß big
groß large
Größe size
Großmutter grandmother
Großvater grandfather
grün green
gucken look
Gürtel belt
gut fine (good)
gut good
gutaussehend handsome
guten Tag good day

H

Haarbürste hairbrush
Haare hair
Hafen harbor
hallo hello
hallo hi
Hals throat
Halsbonbon lozenges
Halt stop (n)
haltbar sturdy
halten stop (v)
Hämorrholden hemorrhoids
Hand hand
Handarbeiten handicrafts
Handschuhe gloves
Handtasche purse
Handtuch towel
hart hard
Hase rabbit
häßlich ugly
hassen hate (v)
Haupt main

Haus house
hausgemacht homemade
Haustier pet (n)
Haut skin
Heimweh homesick
heiß hot
Helm helmet
Hemd shirt
Herbst autumn
Herr gentleman
Herr Mr.
Herren men
Herz heart
heute today
heute abend tonight
hier here
Hilfe help (n)
Himmel heaven
Himmel sky
Hinfahrkarte one way (ticket)
hinter behind
Hitze heat (n)
Hobby hobby
hoch high
hoch tall
hoch up
Hochzeit wedding
Hochzeitsreise honeymoon
Höhle cave
Holz wood
hören hear
Hosen pants
Hotel hotel
hübsch pretty
Hügel hill
Hühnchen chicken
Hund dog

hungrig hungry
husten cough (v)
Hustenpastillen cough drops
Hut hat

I

Ich I
Ihr her
Im Freien outdoors
Imbiß snack
Immer always
Importiert imported
In in
Industrie industry
Information information
Ingenieur engineer
Innen inside
Insekt insect
Insel island
Interessant interesting
Ist is
Italien Italy

J

ja yes
Jacke coat
Jacke jacket
Jacke vest
Jahr year
Jahrhundert century
Jeans jeans
jede each
jede every
jetzt now

Jod iodine
Jogging jogging
Jucken itch (n)
Jugendherberge youth hostel
Jugendlicher teenager
jung young
Junge boy

K

Kaffee coffee
Kalender calendar
Kalorie calorie
kalt cold (adj)
Kamm comb (n)
Kanada Canada
Kanal canal
Kanu canoe
Kapitän captain
kaputt broken
Karaffe carafe
Karte card
Karte map
Karten cards (deck)
Karton box
Käse cheese
Kassette cassette
Kassette tape (cassette)
Kassierer cashier
Kathedrale cathedral
Katze cat
kaufen buy
Kaugummi gum
Kaution deposit
Keller basement
Keller cellar

Kellner waiter
Kellnerin waitress
Kerze candle
Kessel kettle
Kette necklace
Kiefer jaw
Kinder children
Kinderbett crib
Kinderstuhl highchair
Kino cinema
Kirche church
Kissen pillow
Klammeraffe stapler
klar clear
Klasse class
Kleid dress (n)
Kleider clothes
Kleiderbügel coat hanger
klein little (adj)
klein small
Kliff cliff
Klimaanlage air-conditioned
Klopapier toilet paper
klug intelligent
Knie knee
Knopf button
kochen cook (v)
Koffer suitcase
komfortabel comfortable
komisch funny
kommen come
kompliziert complicated
Komputer computer
konfirmieren confirm
König king
Königin queen
können can (v)

Konzert concert
Kopf head
Kopfschmerzen headache
Korb basket
Korken cork
Korkenzieher corkscrew
Körper body
kosten cost (v)
krank ill
krank sick
Krankenhaus hospital
Krankheit disease
Kreditkarte credit card
Küche kitchen
Kugelschreiber pen
Kuh cow
kühl cool
Kunst art
Kunstgewerbe crafts
Künstler artist
künstlich artificial
kurz short
Küß kiss
Küste coast

L

Lächeln smile (n)
lachen laugh (v)
Laken bedsheet
Laken sheet
Lamm lamb
Lampe lamp
Land country
Landstraße highway
langsam slow

Lätzchen bib
lau lukewarm
laufen run (v)
laut loud
laut noisy
Leben life
leben live
Lebensmittelgeschäft grocery store
lecker delicious
Leder leather
ledig single
leer empty
Lehrer teacher
Leihbücherei library
leihen borrow
leihen lend
Leine string
Leiter ladder
Leitungswasser water, tap
letzte last   *(laygen)*
Leute people *lesen*
Licht light (n)   *to read*
lieben love (v)
Liebhaber lover
Lied song
Liege cot
links left
Lippe lip
Liste list
Liter liter
Loch hole
Löffel spoon
Luft air
Luftpost air mail
Lungen lungs

M

machen make (v)
macho macho
Mädchen girl
Magen stomach
Mann man
männlich male
Markt market
Maximum maximum
Medikamente medicine
Meer ocean
Meer sea
Meeresfrüchte seafood
mehr more
mein Herr sir
mein my
Menge crowd (n)
merkwürdig strange
Messer knife
Metall metal
mieten rent (v)
Mineralwasser mineral water
Minimum minimum
Minuten minutes
Mischung mix (n)
Mißverständnis
    misunderstanding
mit by (via)
mit with
mitnehmen take out (food)
Mittag noon
mittel medium
Mitternacht midnight
Mittwoch Wednesday
Möbel furniture

möchte want
Mode fashion
modern modern
mögen like (v)
möglich possible
Moment moment
Monat month
Mond moon
Montag Monday
Morgen morning
morgen tomorrow
Mücke mosquito
Mückenspray insect repellant
müde tired
Mund mouth
Münzen coins
Museum museum
Musik music
Muskel muscle
Mutter mother
MWST TAX

N

nach after
nach to
nachher afterwards
Nachmittag afternoon
Nachricht message
nachschenken refill (v)
nächste next
Nacht night
Nachtisch dessert
nackt naked
Nadel needle
Nadel pin
Nagelschere nail clipper

DICTIONARY

nahe near
Name name
naß wet
Nase nose
Nationalität nationality
Natur nature
natürlich natural
Nebel fog
Neffe nephew
nehmen take
nein no
nervös nervous
nett nice
neu new
nicht not
Nichte niece
Nichtraucher non-smoking
nichts nothing
nie never
niedrig low
Niesen sneeze (n)
noch ein another
noch einmal again
noch einmal repeat
Norden north
normal normal
Notizbuch notebook
notwendig necessary
null zero
nur only
nutzen use

O

O.K. O.K.
ob if

oben upstairs
Obst fruit
oder or
Ofen oven
offen open (adj)
öffentlich public
öffnen open (v)
ohne without
Ohr ear
Ohrenschützer earplugs
Ohrringe earrings
Onkel uncle
Oper opera
Optiker optician
orange orange (color)
Original original
örtlich local
Osten east
Ostern Easter
Österreich Austria

P

Paket package
Papa dad
Papier paper
Parfum perfume
Park park (garden)
parken park (v)
Party party
Paß passport
peinlich embarrassing
per Anhalter fahren hitchhike
perfekt perfect
Periode period (woman's)
Person person

Pferd horse
Pflanze plant
Pflaster band-aid
phantastisch fantastic
Photo photo
Photoapparat camera
Picknick picnic
Pille pill
Pinzette tweezers
Pizza pizza
Plastik plastic
Plastiktüte plastic bag
Platz seat
Platz square (town)
plötzlich suddenly
Polizei police
Post mail (n)
Poster poster
Postkarte postcard
praktisch practical
Präservativ condom
Preis price
Priester priest
privat private
probieren taste (v)
Problem problem
Prost! Cheers!
Prozent percent
Pullover sweater
Puppe doll

Q

Qualität quality

R

Rad wheel
Radiergummi eraser
Radio radio
Rasiercreme shaving cream
Rasierer razor
Rasierwasser aftershave
Rauchen smoking
Rechnung bill (payment)
rechts right
reden talk
Regen rain (n)
Regenbogen rainbow
Regenmantel raincoat
Regenschirm umbrella
reich rich
reif ripe
Reise journey
Reisebüro travel agency
reisen travel
Reisende passenger
Reisescheck traveler's check
Reißverschluß zipper
reiten horse riding
Religion religion
reparieren fix (v)
reparieren repair (v)
reservieren reserve
Reservierung reservation
Rezept prescription
Rezept recipe
Richtung direction
Rindfleisch beef
Ring ring (n)
Rock skirt

roh raw
Rollschuhe roller skates
romantisch romantic
rosa pink
rot red
Rückfahrt roundtrip
Rückgabe refund (n)
Rucksack backpack
Rucksack rucksack
Ruderboot rowboat
Ruhe silence
ruhig quiet
Ruine ruins
runter down

S

Saft juice
Sahne cream
Samstag Saturday
Sandalen sandals
Sänger singer
sauber clean (adj)
sauer sour
Schaffner conductor
Schal scarf
Schale bowl
Schale shell
Scheck check
Scheibe slice
Schenkel thigh
Schere scissors
schicken ship (v)
Schiff boat
Schiff ship (n)
Schild sign

schlafen sleep (v)
schläfrig sleepy
Schlafsaal dormitory
Schlagsahne whipped cream
schlecht bad
schlechter worse
schlechteste worst
Schließfächer lockers
Schloß lock (n)
Schloß palace
schlucken swallow (v)
Schlüssel key
schmal narrow
Schmerz pain
Schmuck jewelry
schmutzig dirty
schnarchen snore
Schnee snow
Schnuller pacifier
Schnurrbart moustache
Schokolade chocolate
schon already
schön beautiful
Schraubenzieher screwdriver
schrecklich horrible
schrecklich terrible
schreiben write
Schuhe shoes
Schule school
Schulter shoulder
schwanger pregnant
Schwanz tail
schwarz black
Schwein pig
Schweinefleisch pork
Schweiz Switzerland
schwer heavy

Schwester sister
Schwiegermutter mother-in-law
Schwiegervater father-in-law
schwierig difficult
Schwierigkeiten trouble
Schwimmbad swimming pool
schwimmen swim
schwitzen sweat (v)
schwul gay
See lake
segeln sailing
sehen see
sehr very
Seide silk
Seife soap
Seil rope
Seite page
Selbstbedienung self-service
senden send
Serviette napkin
Sex sex
sexy sexy
Shampoo shampoo
shorts shorts
sich beeilen hurry (v)
sich beschweren complain
sich erholen relax (v)
sich erinnern remember
sich sonnen sunbathe
sich übergeben vomit (v)
sicher safe
Sicherheitsnadel safety pin
sie she
sie they
Sie you (formal)
Silber silver
singen sing

skilaufen ski (v)
Skulptur sculpture
Socken socks
sofort immediately
sofortig instant
Sohn son
Sommer summer
Sonne sun
Sonnenbrand sunburn
Sonnenbräune suntan (n)
Sonnenbrille sunglasses
Sonnencreme sunscreen
Sonnenöl suntan lotion
Sonnenschein sunshine
Sonnenstich sunstroke
Sonnenuntergang sunset
sonnig sunny
Sonntag Sunday
Spaß fun
spät late
später later
Speisekarte menu
Spezialität specialty
Spiegel mirror
Spiel game
spielen play (v)
Spielzeug toy
Spinne spider
Spitzname nickname
Sport sport
Sprache language
sprechen speak
springen jump (v)
sprudelnd fizzy
Staat state
Stadt city
Stadt town

stark strong
Station station
sterben die
Stern star (in sky)
Steuer tax
Stiefel boots
Stil style
Stimme voice
Stock story (floor)
Stoff cloth
stören disturb
Strand beach
Straße street
Streichhölzer matches
Streik strike (no work)
Streit fight (n)
streiten fight (v)
Stück piece
Student student
Stuhl chair
Stunde hour
Sturm storm
Süden south
sündig scandalous
super great
Supermarkt supermarket
süß sweet
synthetisch synthetic

T

T-Shirt T-shirt
Tag day
Taille waist
Tal valley
Tampons tampons

Tankstelle gas station
Tante aunt
tanzen dance (v)
Tasche pocket
Taschendieb pick-pocket
Taschenlampe flashlight
Taschentuch tissues
Tasse cup
Team team
Telefon telephone
Teller plate
Temperatur temperature
Tennis tennis
Teppich carpet
Teppich rug
Tesafilm scotch tape
teuer expensive
Theater play
Theater theater
Thermometer thermometer
Tier animal
Tipp-Ex white-out
Tisch table
Tochter daughter
Toilette toilet
tot dead
töten kill
Tour tour
Tourist tourist
traditionell traditional
tragen carry
Tragflächenboot hydrofoil
Traum dream (n)
träumen dream (v)
traurig sad
Treppe stairs

trocken dry
Tunnel tunnel
Tür door
Turm tower
Turnschuhe tennis shoes
Tüte bag

U

Übelkeit nausea
über above
Überraschung surprise (n)
übersetzen translate
Uhr watch (n)
Umleitung detour
umsonst free (no cost)
umwickeln wrap
unabhängig independent
und and
Unfall accident
ungefähr approximately
unglaublich incredible
unglücklicher-weise unfortunately
Universität university
unmöglich impossible
uns us
unschuldig innocent
unter below
unter under
Unterhose underpants
Unterhosen briefs
Unterhosen panties
Unterschrift signature
Unterwäsche underwear

V

Vater father
Vegetarier vegetarian (n)
Verabredung appointment
verboten forbidden
verboten prohibited
Verbrennung burn (n)
Verdauungs-störung indigestion
verdorben rotten
Vereinigte Staaten United States
vergessen forget
Vergewaltigung rape (n)
verheiratet married
verkaufen sell
Verkehr traffic
verletzt injured
verloren lost
Vermittlung operator
Versicherung insurance
Verspätung delay
verstehen understand
Verstopfung constipation
Vetter cousin
Video video
Videogerät video recorder
Videokamera video camera
viel much
viele many
vielleicht maybe
Viertel quarter (¼)
violett purple
Virus virus
Visitenkarte business card

Vitamine vitamins
Vogel bird
Völlig total
von from
von of
vor before
Vorfahre ancestor
Vorführung show (n)
vorsichtig careful
Vorspeise appetizers

W

wandern hike
wann when
warm warm (adj)
warten wait
warum why
was what
Waschbecken sink
Wäscheklammern clothes pins
Wäscheleine clothesline
waschen wash
Waschsalon laundromat
Wasser water
Wasserfall waterfall
Wasserhahn faucet
Wechsel change (n)
Wechsel exchange (n)
wechseln change (v)
Wecker alarm clock
weiblich female
Weihnachten Christmas
weil because
Wein wine
Weinberg vineyard

weinen cry (v)
weiß white
weit far
Welt world
wenig few
wer who
werfen throw
Westen west
Wetter weather
Wettervorhersage weather forecast
wichtig important
wie how
wie schade pity, it's a
wieviel kostet how much ($)
wieviele how many
wild wild
willkommen welcome
Wind wind
Windel diaper
Winter winter
wir we
Wischtücher handiwipes
wissen know
Wissenschaft science
Wissenschaftler scientist
Witwe widow
Witwer widower
Witz joke (n)
wo where
Woche week
Wohnung apartment
Wohnwagen R.V.
Wolle wool
Wort word
Wörterbuch dictionary
wünschen wish (v)

wütend angry
wütend mad

Z

Zahn tooth
Zahnarzt dentist
Zahnbürste toothbrush
Zahnpasta toothpaste
Zahnseide dental floss
Zahnstocher toothpick
Zange pliers
zart tender
Zeh toe
zeigen point (v)
zeigen show (v)
Zeitabschnitt period (of time)
Zeitschrift magazine
Zeitung newspaper
Zelt tent
Zelthäringe tent pegs
Zentrum center
ziehen pull
Zigarette cigarette
Zimmer bedroom
Zimmer room
Zimmer frei vacancy (sign)
Zoo zoo
zu too
Zug train
zuhören listen
Zukunft future
zurückgeben return
zusammen together
Zuschlag supplement

zweite second
zweiter Klasse second class
Zwillinge twins
Zwischenstecker adaptor

Hurdling the Language Barrier

Don't be afraid to communicate

Even the best phrase book won't satisfy your needs in every situation. To really hurdle the language barrier, you need to leap beyond the printed page, and dive into contact with the locals. Never allow your lack of foreign language skills to isolate you from the people and cultures you traveled halfway around the world to experience. Remember that in every country you visit, you're surrounded by expert, native-speaking tutors. Spend bus and train rides letting them teach you.

Start conversations by asking politely in the local language, "Do you speak English?" When you speak English with someone from another country, talk slowly, clearly, and with carefully chosen words. Use what the Voice of America calls "simple English." You're talking to people who are wishing it was written down, hoping to see each letter as it tumbles out of your mouth. Pronounce each letter, avoiding all contractions and slang. For bad examples, listen to other tourists.

Keep things caveman-simple. Make single nouns work as entire sentences ("Photo?"). Use internationally-understood words ("Self-service" works in Bavaria). Butcher the language if you must. The important thing is to make the effort. To get air mail stamps, you can flap your wings and say "tweet, tweet." If you want milk, moo and pull two imaginary udders. Risk looking like a fool.

If you're short on words, make your picnic a potluck. Pull out a map and point out your journey. Draw what you mean. Bring photos from home and introduce your family. Play cards or toss a Frisbee. Fold an origami bird for kids or dazzle 'em with sleight-of-hand magic.

Go ahead and make educated guesses. Many situations are easy-to-fake multiple choice questions. Practice. Read timetables, concert posters and newspaper headlines. Listen to each language on a multilingual tour. Be melodramatic. Exaggerate the local accent. Self-consciousness is the deadliest communication-killer.

Choose multilingual people to communicate with, like students, business people, urbanites, young well-dressed people, or anyone in the tourist trade. Use a small note pad to keep track of handy phrases you pick up—and to help you communicate more clearly with the locals by scribbling down numbers, maps, and so on. Some travelers carry important messages written on a small card: vegetarian, boiled water, your finest ice cream.

Numbers and Stumblers:

■ Europeans write a few numbers differently than we do. The one has an upswing (1), the four looks like a lightning bolt (4), and the seven has a cross (7).

■ Europeans write the date in this order: day/month/year. Christmas is 25-12-01, not 12-25-01.

■ Commas are decimal points and decimals are commas. A dollar and a half is 1,50 and 5.280 feet are in a mile.

■ The European "first floor" isn't the ground floor, but the first floor up.

■ When counting with your fingers, start with your thumb. If you hold up only your first finger, you'll probably get two of something.

International words

As our world shrinks, more and more words hop across their linguistic boundaries and become international. Savvy travelers develop a knack for choosing words most likely to be universally understood ("auto" instead of "car," "kaput" rather than "broken," "photo," not "picture"). Internationalize your pronunciation. "University," if you play around with its sound (oo-nee-vehr-see-tay), will be understood anywhere. Practice speaking English with a heavy German accent. Wave your arms a lot. Be creative.

Here are a few internationally understood words. Remember, cut out the Yankee accent and give each word a pan-European sound.

Stop	Kaput	Vino	Restaurant
Ciao	Bank	Hotel	Bye-bye
Rock 'n roll	Post	Camping	OK
Auto	Picnic	Amigo	Autobus (boos)
Nuclear	Macho	Tourist	English
Yankee	Americano	Mama mia	Michelangelo
Beer	Oo la la	Coffee	Casanova (romantic)
Chocolate	Moment	Sexy	Disneyland
Tea	Coca-Cola	No problem	Passport
Telephone	Photo	Photocopy	Police
Europa	Self-service	Toilet	Information
Super	Taxi	Central	Rambo
Pardon	University	Fascist	U.S. profanity

German tongue twisters:

Tongue twisters are a great way to practice a language—and break the ice with the locals. Here are a few *Zungenbrecher* that are sure to challenge you, and amuse your hosts:

Zehn zahme Ziegen zogen Zucker zum Zoo.

Ten domesticated goats pulled sugar to the zoo.

Blaukraut bleibt Blaukraut und Brautkleid bleibt Brautkleid.

Bluegrass remains bluegrass and a wedding dress remains a wedding dress.

Fischer's Fritze fischt frische Fische, frische Fische fischt Fischer's Fritze.

Fritz Fischer catches fresh fish, fresh fish Fritz Fisher catches.

Die Katze trapst die Treppe rauf.

The cat is walking up the stairs.

Ich komme über Oberammergau, oder komme ich über Unterammergau?

I am coming via Oberammergau, or am I coming via Unterammergau?

English tongue twisters:
After your German friends have laughed at you, let them try these tongue twisters in English:

If neither he sells seashells, nor she sells seashells, who shall sell seashells? Shall seashells be sold?	Wenn er keine Muscheln verkauft, und sie verkauft keine Muscheln, wer verkauft dann Muscheln, Werden Muscheln verkauft?
Peter Piper picked a peck of pickled peppers.	Peter Pfeiffer erntete einen Korb voll eingemachter Pfefferschoten.
Rugged rubber baby buggy bumpers.	Starke Gummistoßdämpfer am Kinderwagen.
The sixth sick sheik's sixth sheep's sick.	Das sechste Schaf vom sechsten Scheich ist krank.
Red bug's blood and black bug's blood.	Blut vom roten Käfer und Blut vom schwarzen Käfer.
Soldiers' shoulders.	Soldatenschultern.
Thieves seize skis.	Diebe klauen Schi.
I'm a pleasant mother pheasant plucker. I pluck mother pheasants. I'm the most pleasant mother pheasant plucker that ever plucked a mother pheasant.	Ich bin eine freundliche Federrupferin von Fasanenhennen. Ich rupfe Federn von Fasanenhennen. Ich bin die freundlichste Federrupferin von Fasanenhennen, die je die Federn einer Fasanenhenne gerupft hat.

Let's Talk Telephones

Smart travelers use the telephone every day to make hotel reservations, check on tourist information, or call home. The card-operated public phones are easier to use than coin-operated phones. Buy a *Telefonkarte* (telephone card) at any European post office or newsstand. Your *Telefonkarte* will work for local, long distance, and international calls made from card-operated pay phones throughout the country where you purchase your card.

Hotel room phones can be reasonable for local calls, but a terrible rip-off for long-distance calls. To avoid hassles, make your calls from a public phone or the post office.

European time is six/nine hours ahead of the east/west coast of the United States. Breakfast in Berlin is midnight in California.

Dialing Direct

Calling Between Countries: Dial the international access code (usually 00 for most European countries, 011 for America), the country code of the country you're calling, the area code (if it it starts with zero, drop the zero), and then the local number.

Calling Long Distance Within a Country: First dial the area code (including its zero), then the local number.

Europe's Exceptions: Some countries do not use area codes, such as Italy, Spain, France, Norway, and Denmark. To make an international call to these countries, dial the international access code (usually 00), the country code, and then the local number in its entirety (okay, so there's one exception; for France, drop the initial zero of the local number). To make long-distance calls within any of these countries, simply dial the local number, whether you're calling across the country or across the street.

International Access Codes

When dialing direct, first dial the international access code of the country you're calling from. For most countries, it's "00." The few exceptions are Spain (07), Sweden (009), and the U.S.A./Canada (011).

Country Codes

After dialing the international access code, dial the code of the country you're calling.

Austria—43	France—33	Netherlands—31
Belgium—32	Germany—49	Norway—47
Britain—44	Greece—30	Portugal—351
Czech Rep.—420	Ireland—353	Spain—34
Denmark—45	Italy—39	Sweden—46
Estonia—372	Latvia—371	Switzerland—41
Finland—358	Lithuania—370	U.S.A./Canada—1

U.S.A. Direct Services: Calling Card Operators

It's cheaper to call direct, but if you have a calling card and prefer to have an English-speaking operator dial for you, here are the numbers:

	AT&T	MCI	SPRINT
Austria	022-903-011	022-903-012	022-903-014
Germany	0130-0010	0800-888-8000	0130-0013
Switzerland	0800-89-0011	0800-89-0222	0800-89-9777
Czech Rep.	00420-00101	00420-00112	00420-87187

Weather

First line is average daily low (°F); second line average daily high (°F); third line, days of no rain.

	J	F	M	A	M	J	J	A	S	O	N	D
GERMANY	29	31	35	41	48	53	56	55	51	43	36	31
Frankfurt	37	42	49	58	67	72	75	74	67	56	45	39
	22	19	22	21	22	21	21	21	21	22	21	20
AUSTRIA	26	28	34	41	50	56	59	58	52	44	36	30
Vienna	34	38	47	57	66	71	75	73	66	55	44	37
	23	21	24	21	22	21	22	21	23	23	22	22
SWITZ.	29	30	35	41	48	55	58	57	52	44	37	31
Geneva	39	43	51	58	66	73	77	76	69	58	47	40
	20	19	21	19	19	19	22	21	20	20	19	21

Metric conversions (approximate)

1 inch = 25 millimeters   1 foot = .3 meter
1 yard = .9 meter   1 mile = 1.6 kilometers
1 sq. yard = .8 sq. meter   1 acre = 0.4 hectare
1 quart = .95 liter 1 ounce = 28 grams
1 pound = .45 kilo   1 kilo = 2.2 pounds
1 centimeter = 0.4 inch   1 meter = 39.4 inches
1 kilometer = .62 mile
Miles = kilometers divided by 2 plus 10%
(120 km ÷ 2 = 60, 60 +12 = 72 miles)
Fahrenheit degrees = double Celsius + 30
32° F = 0° C, 82° F = about 28° C

APPENDIX

Faxing your hotel reservation

Most hotel managers know basic "hotel English."
Photocopy and enlarge this form, then fax away.

....

One page fax   My fax #:_____

To: Today's date: ___ / ___ / ___
From: day month year

Dear Hotel _____,
    Please make this reservation for me:

Name: _____

Total # of people: ____ # of rooms: ____ # of nights: ____

Arriving: ___ / ___ / ___   Time of arrival (24-hour clock): _____
          day month year   (I will telephone if later)

Departing: ___ / ___ / ___
           day month year

Room(s): Single Double Twin   Triple   Quad   Quint
With: Toilet Shower   Bathtub   Sink only
Special needs: View   Quiet   Cheapest room   Ground floor

Credit card: Visa   Mastercard   American Express

Card #: _____ Exp. date: _____

Name on card: _____

If a deposit is necessary, you may charge me for the first night. Please fax
or mail me confirmation of my reservation, along with the type of room
reserved, the price, and whether the price includes breakfast. Thank you.

Signature: _____
Name: _____
Address :_____
Phone: _____ E-mail: _____

Your tear-out cheat sheet

Good day.	**Guten Tag.**	**goo**-ten tahg
Do you speak English?	**Sprechen Sie Englisch?**	**shprekh**-en zee **eng**-lish
Yes. / No.	**Ja. / Nein.**	yah / nīn
I don't speak German.	**Ich spreche kein Deutsch.**	ikh **shprekh**-eh kīn doych
Excuse me.	**Entschuldigung.**	ent-**shool**-dee-goong
I'm sorry.	**Es tut mir leid.**	es toot meer līt
Please. / Thank you.	**Bitte. / Danke.**	**bit**-teh / **dahng**-keh
No problem.	**Kein Problem.**	kīn proh-**blaym**
Very good.	**Sehr gut.**	zehr goot
You are very kind.	**Sie sind sehr freundlich.**	zee zint zehr **froynd**-likh
Goodbye.	**Auf Wiedersehen.**	owf **vee**-der-zayn
Where is...?	**Wo ist...?**	voh ist
...a hotel	**...ein Hotel**	īn hoh-**tel**
...a youth hostel	**...eine Jugend-herberge**	ī-neh **yoo**-gend-hehr-behr-geh
...a restaurant	**...ein Restaurant**	īn res-tow-**rahnt**
...a supermarket	**...ein Supermarkt**	īn **zoo**-per-markt
...a pharmacy	**...eine Apotheke**	ī-neh ah-poh-**tay**-keh
...a bank	**...eine Bank**	ī-neh bahnk
...the train station	**...der Bahnhof**	dehr **bahn**-hohf
...the tourist information office	**...das Touristen-informationsbüro**	dahs **too**-ris-ten-in-for-maht-see-ohns-**bew**-roh
...the toilet	**...die Toilette**	dee toh-**leh**-teh
men / women	**Herren / Damen**	**hehr**-ren / **dah**-men
How much is it?	**Wieviel kostet das?**	vee-**feel kos**-tet dahs
Write it?	**Schreiben?**	**shrī**-ben

Cheap / Cheaper / Cheapest.	Billig / Billiger / Am Billigsten.	**bil**-lig / **bil**-lig-er / ahm **bil**-lig-sten
Is it free?	Ist es umsonst?	ist es oom-**zohnst**
Included?	Inklusive?	in-**kloo**-sev
Do you have...?	Haben Sie...?	**hah**-ben zee
Where can I buy...?	Wo kann ich kaufen?	voh kahn ikh **kow**-fen
I would like...	Ich hätte gern...	ikh **het**-teh gehrn
We would like...	Wir hätten gern...	veer **het**-ten gehrn
...this.	...dies.	deez
...just a little.	...nur ein bißchen.	noor īn **bis**-yen
...more.	...mehr.	mehr
...a ticket.	...ein Karte.	īn **kar**-teh
...a room.	...ein Zimmer.	īn **tsim**-mer
...the bill.	...die Rechnung.	dee **rekh**-noong

one	eins	īns
two	zwei	tsvī
three	drei	drī
four	vier	feer
five	fünf	fewnf
six	sechs	zex
seven	sieben	**zee**-ben
eight	acht	ahkht
nine	neun	noyn
ten	zehn	tsayn

At what time?	Um wieviel Uhr?	oom vee-**feel** oor
Just a moment.	Moment.	moh-**ment**
now / soon / later	jetzt / bald / später	yetzt / bahld / **shpay**-ter
today / tomorrow	heute / morgen	**hoy**-teh / **mor**-gen

Rick Steves' Europe Through the Back Door Catalog

All of these items have been especially designed for independent budget travelers. They have been thoroughly field tested by Rick Steves and his globe-trotting ETBD staff, and are completely guaranteed. Prices include a free subscription to Rick's quarterly travel newsletter.

Back Door Bag convertible suitcase/backpack $75

 At 9"x21"x13" this specially-designed, sturdy, functional bag is maximum carry-on-the-plane size (fits under the seat), and your key to foot-loose and fancy-free travel. Made in the USA from rugged, water-resistant 1000 denier Cordura nylon, it converts from a smart-looking suitcase to a handy backpack. It has hide-away padded shoulder straps, top and side handles, and a detachable shoulder strap (for toting as a suitcase). Beefy, lockable perimeter zippers allow easy access to the roomy (2500 cubic inches) main compartment. Two large outside pockets are perfect for frequently used items. A nylon stuff bag is also included. Over 50,000 Back Door travelers have used these bags around the world. Rick Steves helped design this bag, and lives out of it for 3 months at a time. Comparable bags cost much more. Available in black, navy blue and très chic forest green.

European railpasses

...cost the same everywhere, but only ETBD gives you a free hour-long "How to get the most out of your railpass" video, free advice on your itinerary, and your choice of one of Rick Steves' 13 country guidebooks or phrase books. For starters, call 425/771-8303, and we'll send you a free copy of Rick Steves' Annual Guide to European Railpasses.

Moneybelt $8

Absolutely required no matter where you're traveling! An ultra-light, sturdy, under-the-pants, one-size-fits-all nylon pouch, our svelte moneybelt is just the right size to carry your passport, airline tickets and traveler's checks comfortably. Made to ETBD's exacting specifications, this moneybelt is your best defense against theft—when you wear it, feeling a street urchin's hand in your pocket becomes just another interesting cultural experience.

Prices are good through 2000—maybe longer. Orders will be processed within 2 weeks. Call us at (425) 771-8303 or go to www.ricksteves.com for details on shipping/handling charges and local sales tax. Send your check to:

Rick Steves' Europe Through the Back Door
130 Fourth Ave. N, PO Box 2009
Edmonds, WA 98020

www.ricksteves.com

More books by Rick Steves...

Now more than ever, travelers are determined to get the most out of every mile, minute and dollar. Rick will help you have a better trip because you're on a budget, not in spite of it. Each of these books is published by John Muir Publications, and is available through your local bookstore, or through Rick's free newsletter.

Rick Steves' Germany, Austria & Switzerland (with Prague)

For a successful trip, raw information isn't enough. In his country and city guidebooks, Rick weeds through each region's endless possibilities to give you candid, straightforward advice on what to see, where to sleep, how to manage your time, and how to get the most out of every dollar. Besides Germany, Austria & Switzerland (with Prague), the series includes....

Rick Steves' Best of Europe
Rick Steves' Italy
Rick Steves' France, Belgium & the Netherlands
Rick Steves' Paris
Rick Steves' Great Britain & Ireland
Rick Steves' London
Rick Steves' Scandinavia
Rick Steves' Spain & Portugal
Rick Steves' Russia & the Baltics

Rick Steves' Europe Through The Back Door

Updated every year, *ETBD* has given thousands of people the skills and confidence they needed to travel through the less-touristed "back doors" of Europe. You'll find chapters on packing, itinerary-planning, transportation, finding rooms, travel photography, keeping safe and healthy, plus chapters on Rick's favorite back door discoveries.

Mona Winks: Self-Guided Tours of Europe's Top Museums

Let's face it, museums can ruin a good vacation. But *Mona* takes you by the hand, giving you fun and easy-to-follow self-guided tours through Europe's 20 most frightening and exhausting museums and cultural obligations. Packed with more than 200 maps and illustrations.

Europe 101: History and Art for the Traveler

A lively, entertaining crash course in European history and art, *Europe 101* is the perfect way to prepare yourself for the rich cultural smorgasbord that awaits you.

Rick Steves' Postcards from Europe

For twenty-five years Rick Steves has been exploring Europe, sharing his tricks and discoveries in guidebooks and on TV. Now, in *Postcards from Europe* he shares his favorite personal travel stories and his off-beat European friends – all told in that funny, down-to-earth style that makes Rick his Mom's favorite guidebook writer.

Rick Steves' European Phrase Books: French, Italian, German, Spanish/Portuguese, and French/Italian/German

Finally, a series of phrase books written especially for the budget traveler! Each book gives you the words and phrases you need to communicate with the locals about room-finding, food, health and transportation—all spiced with Rick Steves' travel tips, and his unique blend of down-to-earth practicality and humor.

What we do at Europe Through the Back Door

At ETBD we value travel as a powerful way to better understand and contribute to the world in which we live. Our mission at ETBD is to equip travelers with the confidence and skills necessary to travel through Europe independently, economically, and in a way that is culturally broadening. To accomplish this, we:

■ Teach budget European travel skills seminars;
■ Research and write guidebooks to Europe;
■ Write and host a public television series;
■ Sell European railpasses, our favorite guidebooks, travel videos, bags, and accessories;
■ Provide European travel consulting services;
■ Organize and lead free-spirited no-grumps small-group Back Door tours of Europe;
■ Sponsor our European Travel Resource Center near Seattle, and our Web site at www.ricksteves.com

...and we travel a lot.

Back Door 'Best of Europe' tours

If you like our independent travel philosophy but would like to benefit from the camaraderie and efficiency of group travel, our Back Door tours may be right up your alley. Every year we lead friendly, intimate 'Best of Europe' tours, free-spirited 'Bus, Bed & Breakfast' tours, and regional tours of France, Italy, Britain, Ireland, Germany-Austria-Switzerland, Spain-Portugal, Scandinavia, and Turkey. For details, call 425/771-8303 or go to www.ricksteves.com and ask for our free tour booklet.